A GOD WHO SPEAKS

A God Who Speaks

Jacques Guillet

Translated by
Edmond Bonin

GILL AND MACMILLAN

First published 1979
Gill and Macmillan Ltd
15/17 Eden Quay
Dublin 1
with associated companies in
London, New York, Delhi, Hong Kong,
Singapore, Tokyo

Originally published under the title
Un Dieu qui parle, © 1977,
Desclée De Brouwer/Bellarmin, Paris, France.

Copyright © 1979 by The Missionary Society
of St. Paul the Apostle
in the State of New York

Excepts from *The Jerusalem Bible,*
copyright © 1966, Darton, Longman & Todd, Ltd. and
Doubleday & Company, Inc.
Reprinted by permission of the publisher.

7171 1007 9

Printed and bound in Great Britain by
Redwood Burn Limited
Trowbridge & Esher

Contents

Foreword: *Does God Speak?*	1
1. A God Who Speaks: *The Experience of Abraham*	3
Does God Speak?	3
God Said to Abraham	5
2. God Speaks in His Covenant: *The Law of Moses*	11
A Structure: the Covenant	13
Law in the Covenant	16
Word, History and Promise	19
God's Word and Love	21
3. God Speaks Through Men: *The Prophets*	23
The Experiences of Amos	24
The Prophet as Administrator of Justice	30
Utterances—Divine and Human	32
4. God Speaks in Those Who Speak to Him: *The Prayers of the Bible*	35
Peter's Profession of Faith at Caesarea	37
God's Word in Peter	42
Prayer in the Bible: God's Word	45

5. **Jesus Christ, The Word of God** — 49
   The Word Made Flesh — 49
   God Speaks Through the Prophets and in His Son — 51
   The Word: a Living Being — 53
   The Free Word — 55
   Word and Text — 56

6. **The Word and Scripture** — 61
   The Word and Scripture — 62
   Inspired Writings — 67
   Your Word, O Lord, Is Truth — 69

7. **The Word of God and the Church** — 71
   The Church Hears the Word — 72
   The Church Where We Hear the Word — 74
   The Gospels and the Word of God — 76
   The Church and the Gospel — 80

8. **The Word and the Sacrament of Reconciliation** — 83
   The Initial Gift: Forgiveness — 83
   From Christ-as-Sacrament to the Sacraments of Christ — 86

9. **Where Does God Speak?** — 89
   Outside Scripture and the Sacraments — 89
   A God Who Speaks — 90

Appendix: *To Get the Most Out of this Book* — 95
   A. Important Books on the Subject — 95
   B. Guidelines for Individual or Group Study — 96
   C. How All This Changes Our Life Today — 99

Foreword
Does God Speak?

"The Word of God! The Word of God!" In churches and Christian assemblies, this refrain rings out at the drop of a hat, and one wonders whether those who repeat it so readily are aware of what they are saying. They open "the Word of God" at a page chosen beforehand or hit upon at random. They read a few lines and solemnly proclaim them to be "the Word of God." In their daily encounters, they try to pinpoint the fleeting details through which they feel sure God has spoken, and they make crucial decisions because they have received "a Word of God."

Conversely, for many others, who are neither less sincere nor less exacting, "the Word of God" is but an empty phrase which belies both the truth of God and the truth of human experience. Just as God does not have hands or feet, so neither does He have a tongue or a mouth, and one of His essential characteristics is silence. No one has ever seen God, and anyone who claims to have looked upon His face proves he simply does not know what he is talking about. Why should it be otherwise with anyone who imagines he has heard Him? God remains silent, and this silence alone is worthy of both Him and us. Wishing to make Him speak abases Him to our level and plunges us into childishness. Outworn religions may toy with such fables, but modern man wants the truth. What truth can there be in such puerile formulas?

Undoubtedly both sides are right. Our task is to see why. Why do some Christians spontaneously identify Scripture, or a mere quotation from it, with the Word of God? Why do some dedicated Christians insist on detecting the Word of God in their life and activity? Why are others chiefly aware of His silence and afraid of the fuss being made about the whole matter?

This deliberately brief book will not attempt to treat such questions theoretically or furnish precise answers to every possible query. Rather, choosing a few key moments in the Scriptures themselves, it purports to show why faith must of necessity recognize the Word of God; how it can rest on that Word without reducing it to its human expressions; and how it can, in its everyday comportment and outlook on the world, be guided by that light without mistaking it for more or less distorted images.

We shall simply follow the unfolding of the Scriptures, from Genesis to the New Testament, pausing at the decisive crossroads to see how God has spoken in diverse ways and how His Word reaches us today.

1
A God Who Speaks
The Experience of Abraham

Does God Speak?

For Biblical man, one might say God never ceases to speak. "In the beginning . . . God said, 'Let there be light.' " From those first words, which gave rise to creation, down to the last statement of the Book of Revelation, "Now I am making the whole of creation new" (Rev. 21:5), a single refrain resounds from one end of the Scriptures to the other: "God said." To the most multiform writings—patriarchal traditions, prophetic collections, sapiential meditations or psalms, Gospel narratives, or letters from James and Paul—the liturgy solemnly attributes the same majestic title "Word of God." To designate the Christian religion, we commonly speak of "revelation," implying that faith consists in receiving a word and a message from God. Whence this insistence of ours that God should speak? And what do we mean when we so generously attribute speech to Him?

The Heavens Declare

Might this not be an evocative but easily exaggerated concept? The spectacle of the world and nature, for instance, could move one to say that God speaks. For there are landscapes that colloquize, significant events that warn or remind us, voices that reach us in silence. Just as Hiroshima and Auschwitz or the naves of Bourges and the capitals of Autun have something to tell us about their creators and their world, so too, through the universe and its dimensions, a believer may feel himself apostrophized, discover a creative force, sense something like an intention and a language. If he holds that God is at the origin of all things, this is indeed what he is maintaining: that someone—God—wants this world and lets us know He wants it. In this sense and in a certain manner, it is true to say God speaks.

That, however, is not the manner the Bible seems to mean. Here, God holds forth at every instant to say things absolutely beyond nature at its most suggestive or events of the greatest significance. Auschwitz and Bourges tell us of what we already know more or less confusedly; they broaden and deepen our experience of man's cruelty and courage, of his defiance and creativity. We can hear them because, with extraordinary intensity and vividness, they speak our own language—the language of our failures and ignominies, of our successes and triumphs. These works speak; men speak to us through them.

God or the Heavens?

Now, when we think we hear God speak to us in nature, are we really hearing another language? God is the Other, the Wholly Other, and we cannot claim to recognize His voice. What right have we to maintain He is speaking to us? All we may affirm is that, in the world around us, there is a power of expression, a call and the expectation of a meaning. Psalm 19 (1–4) conveys this impression well:

> The heavens declare the glory of God,
> the vault of heaven proclaims his handiwork;
> day discourses of it to day,
> night to night hands on the knowledge.
> No utterance at all, no speech,
> no sound that anyone can hear;
> yet their voice goes out through all the earth,
> and their message to the ends of the world.

Poetic fluency and intellectual precision blend perfectly: creation tells humankind something—something which does not speak but can nevertheless be said and understood; something which, expressed in human language, tells and sings of Another, God. But God Himself does not speak; He is the one about whom and for whom things converse and sing. Neither the song of the universe nor the voice of man is really the word of God. How, then, can the Bible have us hear the word of God on every page?

God Said to Abraham

"Leave your country, your family and your father's house, for the land I will show you. I will make you a great nation; I will bless you and make your name so famous that it will be used as a blessing" (Gen. 12:1–2). The introductory words are explicit: "God said." If they are to be taken seriously, we therefore have here a word from God. What does that mean?

No doubt we would do well to start by establishing what the account does not claim to say. It does not pass itself off as the transcript of an experience; nor does it describe how Abraham was reached—whether by a vision, by some exceptional phenomenon, or simply through a series of reflections, or again in the wake of an event or situation where he could not help acknowledging some sign of God. The text allows of all these possibilities but favors none. Though such discretion may surprise us, it is on the contrary quite natural. The event recorded harks back to a very ancient family tradition, itself garnered only centuries after, when the tribes of Israel were growing aware of their unity and becoming a nation. Later, it is true, the prophets would disclose a few brief personal experiences to their disciples; but in the foundation narratives, such a thing was unheard of, and any wish to force it on them would falsify their nature.

The fact remains that they affirm, "God said to Abraham." How believe them, since they derive from a tradition which can in no way be verified and since they know almost nothing about the facts they relate?

Witnesses to an Experience

Quite simply, we must not ask more of them than they say. They limit themselves to stating a few essential points in very sparing terms. This is the language of the tradition or account described as "Yahwistic"—the language in which Israel, under David and Solomon, expressed the substance of its faith and the starting point of its destiny. The narrative asserts that this starting point was Abraham and the word he had received from God. If the tribes of Israel eventually gained possession of Palestine, it was obviously the upshot of all sorts of complex events, but, primarily, it was because God had willed it and promised it to a man, Abraham.

In using the expression "God said," the account sets itself up neither as witness to the initial event nor as witness to the ancestor's personal experience, but as witness to a history whose initiative and success it attributes to God. God it is who has willed the people of David and given them their land.

Now, to be able to say God has willed this result, one must have learned so from God. For it could have been attributed to chance, to circumstances, to ambition, to economics, to rivalries between neighboring powers or—what amounts to the same thing—between their gods. Faith consists, not in ignoring these facts (which hold for all times), but in affirming that through and by means of them the God of Israel was pursuing His plan. Still, a real plan presupposes intention and will; and, to say that this God had such an intention, one needed to receive this information from Him somehow. Faith in an operative God is possible only by adhering to an utterance in which He says what He is doing. That is why the history of Israel begins with a word from God addressed to Abraham.

Was It God Who Was Speaking?

But who can prove it was God who was speaking? Do not all nations consider their destiny the doing of their particular gods? Do not all religions explain their origin by describing some divine deed, a temple to be constructed, a message to transmit? What right, then, do we have to declare that God spoke to Abraham but said nothing to Mohammed or Buddha?

Before answering this question, let us go back to the word received by Abraham and recorded in Genesis. We must not seek in it the direct echo of the personal experience, the still vivid traces of the encounter between God and this man. Instead, we should take the account for what it is: the condensed expression of a very definite and very self-conscious experience—the birth of belief, based on the word of the God of Israel.

This birth was an event which transformed a whole existence. One day, a man still living in the same part of the world where he had been born, where he had his roots and his horizon, his relatives and his habits, where he nurtured his projects and hopes, suddenly set out from that world, leaving behind him his past and renouncing the dream of his future there. He went away; but he did not go alone, severing all bonds and embarking on a happy-go-lucky existence. He kept a wife with him, servants, flocks; he retained all his responsibilities and continued to assume all his duties. Life did not become simpler for him: pastures for his flocks were no easier to find, the seasons no more clement, and the people he had to deal with no more cordial or accommodating. The world Abraham entered into remained a difficult one, where the name of the game was competition, the struggle to survive, the need to be self-sufficient and preserve one's independence. All the hopes held forth in Genesis—whether in the form of divine promises or of oracles delivered by the fathers, from Noah to Jacob—refer to the same objectives: a numerous and vigorous progeny, a rich and well-situated territory, together with freedom of movement and decision. The initial promise to Abraham is no different, but it gives these hopes a magnitude beyond all imagining: a vast people, a land bestowed by God, a blessing which placed the patriarch at the center of the world, at the summit of all nations. Abraham did not have to renounce either what he had in hand at the moment or what he could expect in the future, but he did have to let God take charge of his life and his hope.

Abraham took that step; he left, because he had received a word from God.

It Was Really God

Such a deed may spring from a moment of madness but will peter out fast. Abraham's deed, on the contrary, launched an entire history, and, for those who lived it, this history was directed by God. For who but God could, at the time this history began, take charge of a people? To guarantee a developing nation a territory it might call home, to defend it from neighbors eager to exploit its every weakness, to maintain the fertility of families and herds, to assure it a glorious future—these are things God alone can take upon Himself. What head of a family, pondering the future of its members, is not torn between shimmering dreams and dread of dire realities? Genesis is full of these hopes and fears and the way fathers envision their children's future. It runs the gamut from Noah's outraged curse on Canaan, "the meanest slave" (9:25), through Isaac's grief when tricked into letting his elder son Esau struggle for survival "far from the richness of the earth . ... far from the dew that falls from heaven" (27:39), to Jacob's exaltation as he blessed Joseph, the "fruitful creeper near the spring. . . . Blessings of ancient mountains; bounty of the everlasting hills; may they descend on Joseph's head, on the brow of the dedicated one among his brothers" (49:22, 26). Yet, to have a blessing, God must be present, for He alone can bless. Fathers can transmit life, give their children a name and voice the dreams they entertain for them; but only God can materialize those dreams. Abraham could not have left every form of security behind and entrusted himself to the future unless he had recognized God.

The True God?

Was this God whom Abraham recognized the true God? And if so, was He not the same as the one worshiped by Abraham's neighbors, the Chaldeans, the Aramaeans or the Midianites? They, too, had their gods, and one in particular who was closer and more attentive, to whose care they committed their marches and their hopes. What prerogative made Abraham's the true God? Might not these various gods be the differently refracted figures of the one God?

Without wishing to disregard whatever truth may be offered by the deities of that world and that period, we must note the originality of Abraham's deed and, consequently, of the God on whom he relies. This deed is a rupture, a break not only with a familiar life-style and milieu but with all its roots as well—and, right at the start, the profoundest of them: the world of religion and gods. Some Other has intervened, one who does not invoke higher rank or exceptional power among the gods, but quite simply declares that He is the Other and that it is He. Thus, Abraham's decision does not result from a comparative evaluation; it is the choice of a God who is precisely "incomparable."

Another characteristic of this God also makes Him incomparable: He acknowledges no boundaries and is at home among "all the tribes of the earth" (Gen. 12:3). Even if that expression does not directly designate the whole of mankind (since Abraham remains a man and his activity and influence are limited by his concrete presence and the places where he happens to be), there is already a properly universal trait in this God. He is God at Ur as well as at Bethel; He is the same in Egypt as in Palestine; He is at home everywhere. That is why He can evict Abraham from his home: He is capable of making him at home anywhere.

This God Speaks

What God does with Abraham consists exactly in *speaking*. To cause someone to perform such actions, to have him topsy-turvy his whole life and that of his household, while yet remaining a free and responsible man—this necessarily involves speaking to him. Without allowing us to imagine one type of experience versus another and without in any way describing the inner meeting, the Biblical account can truly say that God spoke to Abraham. For Abraham was in the presence of Someone capable of making Himself recognized and heard, Someone with an idea and the ability to communicate it, Someone who could reach Abraham and make Himself understood by him, Someone with no need to utter words or speak a language, but whose plans and purposes Abraham could express in his own language, rightfully saying, "God has spoken to me." Without that word, Abraham would be nothing in history. If Abraham matters, it is because God spoke to him.

The first word is a call: it speaks to the inmost heart and requires total commitment. It presupposes between man and God an invisible and essential bond, a communication which, for all its immediacy, leaves him entirely himself, making his own decisions, responsible for his deeds, acting in the world. If God speaks to man, it is because He does not allow Himself to go over his head, because He needs man's intelligence and adherence, and because He awaits a reply.

2
God Speaks in His Covenant
The Law of Moses

The Law, Word of God

Among all the "Words of God" in the Old Testament, those formulating laws and commandments occupy a considerable place. Numerically, first of all: a multitude of precepts are expressed either in the imperative or in the future indicative—a still more categorical form, as in "You shall have no gods except me" or "You shall not kill." The voice speaking here is the very voice of God; and what it says is of capital importance precisely because it comes from God, who stakes all His authority on His commandments. Israel has been given its Law through Moses, but he is only a mediator, whose role consists in listening to God's communications and then transmitting them to His people. Several episodes in Exodus picture Moses traveling back and forth between God, present behind the clouds and lightning of Sinai, and the tribes gathered at the foot of the mountain (Ex. 19:9–25; 24:12–15; 34:29–35). When he returns from the summit, Moses has in his hands "the two tablets of the Testimony, tablets of stone inscribed by the finger of God" (Ex.

31:18; 34:29), and for centuries these tablets will constitute the heart of Israel's religious life. To shelter and transport them through the desert, Moses, at God's behest, orders the ark of the covenant built along with a sanctuary where the God of Israel comes to dwell among His people. In all these descriptions, of course, we must make allowance for the necessarily symbolic language devised to retell God's deeds, but we would annihilate the whole of Biblical faith were we to ignore its fundamental assertion: the Law of Israel is the word of God.

Merely a Manner of Speaking?

How is this possible, and what can such an assertion mean? That a man should feel called by God to perform an act which alters his entire existence; that a prophet who is aware of events should realize God is sending him to show his fellowmen the meaning of what they are living through as well as God's place in it—this is understandable, for it corresponds to experiences which we can ascertain and which recur in the history of mankind. But that the legislation of a whole people, the corpus of its laws and customs, should be presented as a collection of "words of God"—this, in our mind, can only be a manner of speaking, a more or less felicitous way of "sacralizing" existence and bestowing indisputable authority on ancient texts. But elementary reflection suffices to relativize this infantile language.

The answer to this difficult question lies in a closer look at what Biblical tradition calls the Law. For us, a law consists of a body of articles forming a whole. Now, we do indeed find, within the five books attributed to Moses and called the Pentateuch, several series or collections of texts which correspond exactly to articles of law. The difficulty is that these texts are grouped and cited according to principles we do not understand well. At times, there are cohesive series, like the decalogue; at times, more or less unified groupings which nonetheless hold together; and at times, special laws related to narrative episodes. This disorder is easy enough to explain: it reflects the different stages of what we may call "Israelite law," the empirical character of its origin, and vestiges of diverse situations and developments. Such variety is extremely precious, since it proves that this law is not artificial but is, on the contrary, the expression of a concrete nation living a very special history.

Still, this important observation brings up the initial problem even more urgently: how are we to believe that a law so strongly rooted in existence, so dependent on history and its vicissitudes, may yet claim to be a compilation of directives from God?

To understand this, we must rediscover profound structures under the apparent disorder.

A Structure: the Covenant

On at least three occasions it is possible to identify a characteristic structure in connection with typically juridical and legislative texts. In Exodus, the legislative corpus comprising the decalogue and the code of the covenant (Ex. 20–23) is introduced by the proposal of a covenant (Ex. 19:3–8) and followed by a ratification rite (Ex. 24:3–11). In the Book of Joshua, once Palestine had been conquered, "[Joshua] laid down a statute and ordinance for [the people] at Shechem" (Jos. 24:25). The text of this statute is not recorded there, but it may have been the "covenantal code" of Exodus 21–23. In any case, this law is, as at Sinai, preceded by the proposal of a covenant and followed by a ratification rite (Jos. 24:1–24, 26–28). Lastly, Deuteronomy consists of three parts: a historical introduction ending with a presentation of the choice to be made (Deut. 1:1–11, 25 and 11:26–32), a body of laws constituting what is called "the Deuteronomic Code," and finally the ratification rite celebrated between Mount Ebal and Mount Gerizim (Deut. 27). In different styles and on varying scales the same structure appears: a historical retrospect in which God Himself recounts His past activity and its present results, a proposal urging the people to make the decisive choice, a complex of regulations, and a sacred rite sealing the covenant between God and His people. In the two more developed episodes, those in Exodus and Deuteronomy, the legislative section comprises two clearly different parts: one, very homogeneous and very compact (the decalogue); and the other, noticeably longer and more diversified (the code).

The Codes

The codes are so named because they are in the form of legislative and juridical texts. They envisage cases susceptible of litigation and set up a system of sanctions. They presuppose a well-defined social framework, customs in actual use, and authorities charged with seeing that the fixed prescriptions are executed. Here, law is the expression of a social community; it formulates the rules for the functioning of a society. Its authority is that of the group, of its beliefs and reflexes. Its rules carry weight because they spell out what is or is not done. Undoubtedly, social pressure plays a considerable role in the formulation and execution of its articles; but we can gauge the level of this society accurately when we see it forbid the exploiting of poor debtors (Ex. 22:24) or oblige someone to help an enemy whose donkey has collapsed (Ex. 23:5). What is interesting about these codes is precisely that they afford us a glimpse of the daily functioning of Israelite society at different periods.

The Decalogue

There is a considerable difference between the codes and the decalogue. Except for the article on the sabbath, the decalogue does not envision any particular situation, any definite social framework. It does not presuppose any constituted authority or provide sanctions. The commandments are formulated in general and categorical terms and do not deal with details and circumstances. The voice which resounds here is no longer that of some society, nor does its authority derive from matters of course. It speaks from within, lays down absolute rules, and apparently holds good for everyone, whatever group he may belong to. Through the Israelite, it is directed at man, period. If it gains obedience, so much the better; if not, sanctions are not what will restore its authority. The route from code to decalogue is that which goes from law (the expression of the group) to morality (the expression of conscience).

The Site of Freedom

Law and morality are both necessary and necessarily united, as are the decalogue and the code of the covenant. The code is required so that the decalogue may be liveable and efficacious; the decalogue is indispensable so that the functioning of the code may be a human obedience and an adherence through conscience, rather than the result of social pressure. Thus the decalogue-code relationship introduces freedom. Anyone who hears the decalogue knows that he can transgress its commands, knows that he may sometimes escape society's sanctions, knows in short that all depends on him and his choices: he experiences freedom, and so he must assume his responsibilities.

The Covenant

Before the decalogue and the code, there is the proposal of a covenant. Once this proposal has been accepted, the covenant is sealed by a sacred act performed on holy ground reserved to God. Accordingly, God is present at the beginning and at the end of the Law. At the end, His presence is silent: man is the one who speaks in order to voice his commitment and accompany it with sacred actions, though God's presence and acceptance are what make these actions sacred and this commitment definitive. At the beginning, God is the one who speaks.

The proposal of the covenant comes from a person who can

be recognized by His voice, His deeds and His way of acting. This God causes Himself to be called by His name; He has His own traits, His own style. Between man and Him, there is already a common experience, a road traveled together: "You yourselves have seen what I did with the Egyptians, how I carried you on eagle's wings and brought you to myself" (Ex. 19:4). This God has entered into Israel's existence, so that He forms part of its past and its memories. He has entered as its liberator, and this is how He wants to remain there and why He suggests that it become the people distinguished as belonging to Him: "You of all the nations shall be my very own, for all the earth is mine. I will count you a kingdom of priests, a consecrated nation" (Ex. 19:5–6). The past is the pledge of the future: the God who has delivered His people from Egypt can defend them from all perils. He lays down only one condition: "If you obey my voice and hold fast to my covenant." The experience of the past perceived in faith, and confidence in the future founded upon hope, are inseparable from obedience.

Law in the Covenant

The Law Becomes a Word of God's

Thus, from the fact that the Law is introduced into the covenant, between its proposal by God and its ratification celebrated before God, it becomes wholly and entirely God's word. But it does not, for all that, lose its human consistency and singularity. For it is essential that every nation, in order to exist on earth and develop its specific character, should have its own law, the sign of personal autonomy. Only from the moment it possesses its law does Israel exist. This law, in the form of the codes, is composed of particular cases, of experiences which have been compiled and classified. Some of these experiences relate to the history of this individual nation, but scores of them are common to it and many neighboring peoples. In Israel's codes there are numerous articles whose equivalent we find in foreign legislations. This proves only that Israel is a nation in the midst of others and that it borrows its solutions from the culture of its time and milieu. But these borrowings and the options they presuppose are made within the covenant, so that the people for whom they are destined may be the people of Yahweh. Faith in Him, a determination to translate concretely the experiences lived with Him, is what gives these codes their distinctive physiognomy. Calling them "God's Words" is no exaggeration, since their inherent originality truly comes from Him.

God's Use of "I"

More than once, the "I" who calls Israel to the covenant gives these codes their unique tone. "I shall hear their cry"—that of the stranger, the widow and the orphan—is spoken by the same "I" who declared, "I brought you to myself" (Ex. 22:20-22; 19:4). Such cases are exceptional, however; and it would indeed be abnormal if divine words took over and the voice of God drowned out the dialogue through which men compare their experiences and strive to set the rules of their world. But in proportion as these experiences are multiplied and Israel's law grows more complex, so also do references to the God of the covenant become more explicit and frequent. Compared to the codes of Deuteronomy and especially of Leviticus, where God's word is constantly mentioned, the code of the covenant has a profane accent. But we would be misappreciating the action of God if from His silence we inferred His absence.

In the decalogues the divine "I" occurs several times, but at well-defined moments. We find these direct interventions in the articles which oppose "other gods" to "me, Yahweh your God" (Ex. 20:3, 5, 7), and firstly in the initial declaration which grounds the entire series of commandments: "I am Yahweh your God who brought you out of the land of Egypt, out of the house of slavery" (Ex. 20:2). It is precisely this declaration which expressly binds the decalogue to the covenant, the commandments enjoined on Israel to God's liberating act. This God has delivered His people in order to give them the life-style of the ten commandments.

It is, therefore, this "I" who utters all the words of the decalogue; it is He who addresses His partner each time the latter hears the resounding "you" directed at him: "You shall not kill. You shall not commit adultery . . ." (Ex. 20:13). Nevertheless, there must be some reason why this "I" presents Himself in person in the opening articles and is absent from the rest. God does not speak the same way when He demands adoration for Himself alone and when He forbids adultery. When demanding adoration, He speaks in virtue of what He has done, what He has revealed about Himself, what He is and what Israel has learned. When prohibiting murder and the like, He does not unveil His identity but lets it express itself in an unnamed voice. Whoever hears it experiences it both as the voice of another, the bearer of exigencies he himself has not fixed, and yet as rising up from within himself. Its exigencies tell him what he is, what he may not refuse to be without shortchanging himself and destroying something essential within him.

The Passage Through Conscience

This difference between God's presence revealed in the first articles and unnamed in the rest illustrates the difference between moral conscience and religious conscience, together with the proper articulation which the covenant establishes between them. Man does not need God to hear "You shall not kill": it suffices that he let his conscience speak and thus call his freedom into play, since he has the power to listen to his conscience or silence it. But once he has heard the God of the covenant say, "I am Yahweh your God," he never ceases hearing Him when his conscience says, "You shall not kill." The commandments must pass through his conscience so that, in listening to it, he may know that he is a man and that he adheres to the commandment in the name of what he is and of his freedom as a man. But he who knows the God of the covenant discovers that the voice of his conscience is the very voice of that God. Instantly, this voice takes on another resonance: no longer the imperative tone of an unconditional demand, but the tone of a familiar voice, the presence of a look and a call. Instantly, too, all the words of the decalogue and the codes can assume the form of the sole word, the great commandment: "Listen, Israel: Yahweh our God is the one Yahweh. You shall love Yahweh your God with all your heart, with all your soul, with all your strength" (Deut. 6:4–5).

Word, History and Promise

God Shapes History

In order to make itself recognizable to moral conscience through the decalogue, and to Israel's conscience through its codes, God's word first has to become history. All the covenantal formulas open with a historical reminder which is always formulated by God Himself: "You yourselves have seen what I did" (Ex. 19:4; Deut. 29:1; cf. Jos. 24:2). This way of putting on God's tongue the history which is about to follow derives, not from an uncontrolled need to multiply divine utterances, but from a profound reason. The history of Israel differs from that of all other peoples because of its twofold nature. It is a visible history, consisting of events which can be dated and observed; it is susceptible to being recorded and verified; and, like any other history, it is subject to criticism and historical judgment. But at the same time it is a "sacred" history—which in no way connotes that it is more beautiful or edifying than others, but that it is a history whose secret can be revealed by God, because He is the One who has shaped it. Hence, in Israel's Torah, the historical part is as important as the legislative. Hence also, in the Bible, history is seen to be the word of God just as immediately as prophecy or law. Even when there is no mention that God is speaking, when the story is retold by Moses (as in the first chapters of Deuteronomy) or when the narrator remains anonymous (as in Genesis and Exodus), Israelite tradition maintains as a fundamental axiom that the narrator is Moses and that his account is being dictated to him by God. This is a succinct way of stating an essential principle: it is from God that Israel receives both the events which have given it birth and the meaning of those events. If the story of this people is one directed by God, He alone is capable of saying what it is.

God Makes Us Reread History

That does not mean Israel's history is not equally a human history, one which can be explained by human factors, obeying the normal laws of the world and humanity. In these respects, it is similar to all others. Neither does its originality reside in being conducted by God, for the history of each and every nation on earth is also conducted by God. But, in the case of Israel, God has said what He was doing and has revealed the meaning of His guidance—that is to say, He has spoken. He has spoken because His direction was destined to give birth to faith, and because faith cannot be born except from a word given and received. Since Israel's existence rests upon faith, that existence is founded upon God's word.

Every believer can experience this for himself. To believe in God, to attain to faith, is to discover that God is present in one's existence, not as an alien observer or even an interested tour guide, but as the closest of partners, committing Himself unreservedly and putting all His love into it. The day a believer discovers this, he necessarily relates it back to the beginning, to his birth and beyond. If God is with me today and looks at me with such passionate attention, it is because He has been with me from all time. Hearing God tell me today, "I know you" necessarily means hearing Him also tell me, "I have always known you": "Before I formed you in the womb, I knew you" (Jer. 1:5). And, inevitably, it means rereading my own life with Him—rereading it as I listen to Him explain it to me: a life I already knew, but whose secret God now reveals to me; a life He has made and can recount to me, for He is its author.

God's Word and Love

The covenantal word has a global quality: it embraces the whole of existence. God leads us from the very beginning, calls us at each instant and takes charge of our future. He speaks to us in many ways, but does so in order to be at the heart of our life. To this diverse but nevertheless one and global word, He expects a reply in kind. To His explanation of the past, to the story of our life which He discloses to us, the proper response is faith: a thanksgiving which sings of God's deeds, a credo which enumerates and defines them. To His promise that He will take charge of the future, the answer is hope, which has no need of knowing what tomorrow will look like and leaves it to God, not because He is so strong and wise, but because He loves and wants to give. At the center, during this present moment, there is today and its demands, which we must meet immediately. In the first covenantal formulas, the required response is obedience: "If you obey my voice and hold fast to my covenant . . ." (Ex. 19:5). Never will this requirement be lifted, but the prophets and Deuteronomy came to understand that it is exacted by a God who loves, and that obedience is nothing if it is not a response to love. From then on, the covenant is explained by one word: "If Yahweh set his heart on you and chose you, it was not because you outnumbered other peoples; you were the least of all peoples. It was for love of you" (Deut. 7:7–8); and it consists in one word: "You shall love Yahweh your God with all your heart, with all your soul, with all your strength" (Deut. 6:5). The Law of Israel contains thousands of divine words; but, says Jesus, adding to this greatest and first commandment a second which resembles it—"You must love your neighbor as yourself" (Lev. 19:18)—suffices to comprise in two words "the whole Law and the Prophets also" (Mt. 22:39–40).

3
God Speaks Through Men
The Prophets

From the Patriarchs to the Prophets

God spoke to Abraham. Israel's history and faith rest on this fundamental affirmation, but they do not claim to know what the meeting between God and Abraham consisted in. They say only that Abraham staked his life on an experience which we may call a "word" because it comes from someone else, conveys a meaning and can be formulated in human language, and which we must call "a word from God" because no man could ever elicit this response and this kind of faith. The entire history of the patriarchs in Genesis is founded upon a certitude: God has spoken to our fathers; but no attempt is made to define the very experience these men were afforded by God, the way they perceived His word.

The prophets, on the contrary, present themselves openly as the men of God's word and say they have experienced it directly: "The Lord said to me . . . The word of the Lord was addressed to me . . . Thus spoke the Lord . . . The oracle of the Lord . . . " These refrains punctuate their prophetic discourses—often to the point of wearying the reader or listener and awakening critical suspicion. If a prophet repeats so often that his word is the Lord's, may he not be trying to conceal the obvious fact that, on the contrary, a mere man is holding forth? And, in point of fact, the speaker is indeed a man, with his own style, his own techniques, his strengths and his weaknesses. If he nevertheless affirms that his word is God's, what does he mean, and how can he justify his claim?

The Experiences of Amos

Amos is the earliest of the prophets whose oracles and discourses were gathered into a book. But in his language we can easily recognize traditional formulas, solidly constructed patterns adaptable to varying needs. Among them we must certainly include such common expressions as "Thus speaks Yahweh" and "This is the oracle of Yahweh." Of themselves, these phrases teach us nothing about prophetic experience. But, occasionally, Amos tells us far more about himself—for example, in his series of "visions." Here are two of them, the first (7:1–3) and the third (7:7–9):

> This is what the Lord Yahweh showed me:
> it was a swarm of locusts . . .
> They were about to devour all the greenstuff
>   in the land,
> but I said, "Lord Yahweh, forgive, I beg you.
> How can Jacob survive, being so small?"
> And Yahweh relented;
> "This shall not happen," said Yahweh.

> This is what the Lord Yahweh showed me:
> a man standing by a wall,
> plumb-line in hand.
> "What do you see, Amos?" Yahweh asked me.
> "A plumb-line," I said.
> Then the Lord said to me,

"Look, I am going to measure my people Israel by
   plumb-line;
no longer will I overlook their offenses.
The high places of Isaac are going to be ruined,
the sanctuaries of Israel destroyed,
and, sword in hand, I will attack the House of
   Jeroboam."

Not everything is clear in these passages; it is impossible to define the nature or the psychological context of the visions described. What are we dealing with: more or less ecstatic states we could term extraordinary, or mental images so graphic they seem real, or everyday scenes along the road—a cloud of locusts, a mason near a wall—through which the prophet perceives God's immediate presence? Nothing here allows us to settle the question out of hand. Several points are essential, however, and without them the text loses all its meaning.

What Did Amos See?

First, he affirms that he has seen the Lord—to which one is tempted to oppose the fundamental Biblical belief that God is essentially invisible and that seeing Him would mean instant death (Ex. 19:21; 33:20; Jg. 13:22; cf. Deut. 4:12). But when Amos affirms that he has seen the Lord, he does not add a single word to describe Him. Only the action is sketched out; of face, garment or posture nothing is said. Now, that action is not the movement of a body or hand but, rather, the kind which causes a cloud of locusts to loom on the horizon or a plumb-line to hang. At bottom, everything described in these visions belongs to the visible world and is attributable to human imagination. Still, he declares he has seen the Lord, and we have no reason to doubt his word: this plumb-line and these locusts came directly from God, straight from His hands, as it were. Of course, this is merely a manner of speaking which, in point of fact, Amos does not use but which may enlighten us: what he saw placed him in the presence of the Lord, in His immediate presence.

And what he saw elicited an immediate reaction: he threw himself into prayer, begging God to spare His people. There was not a second to lose: another moment, and the earth would have been ravaged. Such is the content of the first vision; that of the second is far more dramatic, for, this time, intercession was useless. We are not told whether Amos tried, like the first time, or whether God prevented him from doing so beforehand. Everything, however, leads us to believe that the vision and God's disallowance of intercession were simultaneous. But if the prophet might no longer plead to ward off the catastrophe, he could yet run and announce it to the people, in the hope that the imminent threat would convert their hearts and that God would thus be moved.

What God's Word Is

We see what God's word is for Amos: it is both the perception of an act which God is in the process of performing and the conviction of having to do something about it, either by praying in an attempt to stop it or by preaching to bring about the conversion of the people. Nothing here obliges us to suppose that God really spoke words from the language of humans. On the contrary, everything suggests that Amos himself found the words to describe his vision. But everything he says is the expression of what he saw and understood, of a vision on the point of becoming an event, an event decided upon and effected by God. There is nothing which more closely resembles a word than such an experience of God; everything here belongs to the order of words: communication, intention, the designation of an object, the call to go forth announcing and speaking. Without God's having had to speak in our fashion, what the prophet perceived was truly a word from God.

When the Lion Roars

When the lion roars, who is not afraid? When the Lord Yahweh has spoken, who would not prophesy?

Other experiences of Amos' seem briefer yet. He has seen nothing and therefore has nothing to describe, but he has heard—not a word to be translated and explained, but the roar of a beast. On two occasions he mentions this experience, and both times his purpose is to interpret it.

The first such experience (1:2) has a lightning-fast quality:

> Yahweh roars from Zion,
> and makes his voice heard from Jerusalem;
> the shepherds' pastures mourn,
> and the crown of Carmel withers.

At one and the same instant, Amos hears the roaring of a wild beast coming from Jerusalem and sees the greenery on Mount Carmel turn brown. As a shepherd, he had heard the terrifying voice of lions in the desert and observed the paralyzed horror it immediately caused among his flocks. Similarly, it suffices that God should make His cry heard in Jerusalem for the entire land to be seized with terror to the farthest boundary. In what this cry consists Amos does not say, and his initial experience escapes us here. Clearly, however, it is an experience of God, the experience holds a meaning, and the meaning can be translated for listeners. Here again, we have a word.

Amos Interprets an Experience

The second experience (3:3–8) is equally brief at the beginning, but, by means of a skillful device, Amos makes this beginning—which has set everything afoot—the conclusion of a carefully constructed development:

> Do two men take the road together
> if they have not planned to do so?

Does the lion roar in the jungle
if no prey has been found?
Does the young lion growl in his lair
if he has captured nothing?
Does the bird fall to the ground
if no trap has been set?
Does the snare spring up from the ground
if nothing has been caught?
Does the trumpet sound in the city
without the populace becoming alarmed?
Does misfortune come to a city
if Yahweh has not sent it?
No more does the Lord Yahweh do anything
without revealing his plans to his servants the prophets.
The lion roars: who can help feeling afraid?
The Lord Yahweh speaks: who can refuse to prophesy?

The Technique of the Sages

In this passage Amos utilizes a technique popular with the "wise." To draw the portrait of some prototype—say, the unbearable woman or the perfect wife (Ecclus. 25:13–26; Prov. 31:10–31) or the true versus the false friend (Ecclus. 6:5–17; 37:1–6)—the devotees of wisdom revel in heaping up expressive comparisons and stringing them along a significant axis. Here, the axis is the link between a remarkable fact and the event it announces—more precisely, between a sinister sign and the catastrophe it represents. With great art, Amos starts with the everyday sight of two men traveling together, moves on to disturbing images of trap and prey, and ultimately builds up to the terrifying vision of a city taken by storm. Masterfully he applies an old and tried technique, for he has listened to the discussions of wise men and retained what he has learned. Others beside him could doubtlessly do the same. But Amos is a prophet and has a message to deliver—which he does in two phases: first, by placing at the end of the series the conclusion he has been preparing, like a final but still general axiom: "If a prophet speaks, it is because God is acting"; and, second, by stating the concrete fact: "I prophesy because Yahweh has spoken."

The Instant at Which God Speaks

The instant at which God speaks is, for Amos, the instant at which he hears the lion roar. No one else perceives it yet, and the flocks go on grazing peacefully. Only he has so keen an ear as to know that the beast is on the move, even now watching its prey. Indeed, there is in the lion's roar something akin to words: not only the voice which makes itself heard, but the sighting of the prey and the certainty of seizing it. Thus the prophet can hear God speak when, one way or another, he receives from God the assurance that He is determined to act.

Communicating the Word

Once he has this assurance, he must communicate it to his people. That is what Amos does in this extract. He it is who has to invent and find words for every detail in its development; and the whole passage is the work of a human author, of a man trying to suggest and thereby define what it means to be a prophet who speaks. From start to finish, this passage is in the words of a man. From start to finish also, his words strive to convey the initial shock, the message to be transmitted. Thus, all the resources of human speech are elicited and animated by the word received from God. What constitutes a prophet is the fact that he both receives the initial experience, God's word, and renders it in human language faithfully enough that the terms used may legitimately be called God's word.

The Prophet as Administrator of Justice

The passage we have just examined concerned the past and Amos' vocation. Immediately after (3:9–11) comes a text announcing the future of Israel:

> Assemble on Samaria's mountain
> and see what great disorder there is in that city,
> what oppression is found inside her.
> They know nothing of fair dealing
> —it is Yahweh who speaks—
> they cram their palaces full by harshness and extortion.
> Therefore, the Lord Yahweh says this:
> An enemy is going to invade the country,
> your power will be brought low,
> your palaces looted.

In the Form of a Trial

This passage is typical of prophetic preaching—not only because of its repetition of the formula "Yahweh speaks" but also because of its construction, which follows the pattern of a court trial: a reading of the charges (disorder, oppression, violence and extortion), attested by witnesses; a summation by the judge, God in person; and the sentencing (an enemy invasion). From the time of Nathan, who came to rebuke David for assassinating his officer Uriah (2 Sam. 12), down to the days of Jesus, who issued the harshest of warnings to the generation which was rejecting Him (Mt. 23:13–36), this criminal trial format is the one spontaneously used by every prophet sent to confront the guilty in Israel with their offenses and the disasters they were leading to. Just as Amos utilized a sapiential model to make his hearers understand the prophetic experience, so here he adopts a time-honored form to make them realize that he comes as an administrator of justice sent to denounce the sin of his people and pass sentence. And just as he began his sapiential enumeration with God's decision to intervene, so now he again prefaces with God's decision the judgment he has come to pronounce—as is clear from the two formulas which explicitly present God as speaking: first, in the arraignment and, then, at the moment of sentencing.

Human Statements . . .

Consequently, just as the whole sapiential development was designed to help hearers grasp the content of God's word perceived by the prophet, so also the juridical development composed by the prophet as administrator of justice is a human work, the work of a man who can look at the present and reflect upon the future. To ensure that the condemnation of Samaria truly comes from God, there is absolutely no need that He have paraded the sins of the city before Amos' eyes or given him a glimpse of the enemy invasion and the sacking of the capital. On the other hand, Amos, aware that his message consists in unveiling the sins of the kingdom and the tragic fate they are preparing, and intent on giving this divine word its concrete content, must surely have opened his eyes to see what was going on and consider what was brewing.

. . . Which Are God's Word

It does not take a prophet to know that Samaria is filled with disorder and oppression, nor does it take a pronouncement from God to say so; but Amos' contemplation of all this violence is governed by his prophetic experience and the message he has been entrusted with. Because he realizes divine judgement has fallen upon Samaria, the prophet, with both eyes wide open, focuses on the guilty city and tries to define the evil gnawing away at it. The judgement he passes on the Samaritans is that of a man endowed with moral sense and capable of observation. But this man is a prophet, and his judgement is wholly and entirely at the service of his mission—that is to say, at the service of God's judgement. That is why his accusation, drawn up in the juridical language of his people and his day, is at the same time a word from God.

The Sentence

Similarly, when Amos proceeds from accusation to sentence and announces that the country will be invaded and the city sacked, we need not presume that he was granted special lights concerning these future events and allowed to preview the unfolding of history. In Amos' day, though the country was at peace and the opulence of those in high places easily made them forget the imminent dangers, any clear-sighted person could assess, on the one hand, the fragility of a prosperity founded upon injustice, and on the other, the ever-growing power and ambition of the Assyrian kings. Beyond a doubt, many of his contemporaries were capable of envisioning a similar future and of saying so. Moreover, Amos' description of the calamity is quite vague and could apply to many other cases. What makes his announcement a prophecy and a word from God, is the fact that he utters it in the name of the Lord, that the impending event is presented as His decision, and that the fatal logic which leads Samaria from corruption to ruin carries His sanction. God is at work in this destiny; the prophet's mission is to say so, and his statement is the word of God Himself.

Utterances—Divine and Human

Poetic Inspiration, Divine Inspiration

Thus, a prophet's dicta are not reproductions or tracings of God's word. They are human pronouncements, made up of human experiences, describing human situations, molded by the rules of a culture, and enhanced by traditional techniques of discourse and dialogue. God's word is not a human superword, a loftier model of speech to serve as guide and framework for prophets.

To designate this passage from divine to human utterance, Christian tradition regularly uses the term *inspiration*—a concept which is often seriously misunderstood. The divine inspiration we mean is only remotely related to inspiration in the ordinary sense of the word—the kind which makes poets and orators.

A poet in search of inspiration stirs up images and rhythms, launches rhymes and carves out silences. Well before his poem has taken shape—indeed, from the moment he gets under way—he is already dealing with forms and working in the domain of language and human speech.

The word of God does not operate directly at that level. Though prophets may often be inspired in the popular sense of the word, and though they may certainly experience this impulsion and go through this toil, their poetic or oratorical inspiration does not constitute divine inspiration. This latter is situated at another depth—properly spiritual.

The Experience of God's Word

Prophets are constituted such by an experience we may rightly call God's word. They become aware that Another—God—is intervening in their lives and calling them to undertake a mission. They must answer by acts which find expression in words. That is because they are replying to a word. Furthermore, their mission consists in speaking, putting into words what comes to them from God. Here again, that is because they have received a word. Prophets cannot disclose their vocation and mission except in the light of God's word. But His word is not the prototype of theirs, which can mirror the endless varieties of human experience and always enjoys the freedom of God. Amos is particularly interesting because, better than some of the other prophets, he allows us to observe the passage from the initial experience and God's word down to their verbalization in human language. This passage takes place in both directions: the prophet's utterance is not only the passing of a God-given experience into that of an author and orator, but it is also the experience of an author placing all his talent, all his resources and all his art at the service of the initial experience of God's word—not so much to express it as exactly as possible (since, once again, it is not a model to be reproduced) but, rather, to respond to it as faithfully as possible, to convey the violence of the call, the determination of the commitment and the certainty of the result.

4

God Speaks in Those Who Speak to Him
The Prayers of the Bible

Prayer in the Bible

An important part of the Bible consists of prayers addressed to God. One of the earliest pieces of Hebrew literature, Deborah's song after the victory at Kishon (Jg. 5), is all atremble not only with the excitement of a very young nation in the process of putting an end to one world and building another, but also with awestruck faith in the power of God. Hardly a historical or prophetic book but contains one or several canticles. The Book of Psalms attests how carefully Israel set down and preserved its treasury of hymns and prayers. Nor should we be astonished at this fidelity: a people endowed with such a capacity for profound feeling and precise, forceful expression would naturally be led to collect and conserve the more notable achievements of its heart and faith.

What is astounding is, not that these pieces were saved along with the other forms which made up Hebrew literature and became the Bible, but that they were saved for the same reason as the rest and that Israel's faith quite simply considered them the Word of God like the rest. The fact that God spoke through Moses and the prophets seems natural: the words of the Law as well as the reproaches and promises of the prophets patently come from elsewhere and, by their very form, postulate the presence of Another. The most one can do is ask whether the speaker is authorized to speak in the name of that Other, but in Israel no one doubts that God can express Himself through the discourses or writings of His spokesmen. The prayers and hymns are an altogether different matter.

When Man Speaks . . .

Here, it is man who speaks, and he does so without a mission, without a message to deliver. Besides, he remains anonymous. Many psalms have been attributed to David, but posteriorly, and almost nothing in the text of the psalms presupposes a singular and personal event. The always remote allusions to some particular fact—the victory of a king, for instance, or the sacking of Jerusalem—all have a collective dimension. These events belong to the history of a people, not of an individual. Even those "royal" psalms meant for the investiture of a new king are designed for any coronation and include no name. The prophetic collections—down to the last of them, the Book of Revelation—all begin by identifying their author: "The word of Yahweh that was addressed to Hosea, son of Beeri" (Hos. 1:1); "The vision of Isaiah, son of Amoz" (Is. 1:1); "From John, to the seven churches of Asia" (Rev. 1:4), for each prophet is personally involved in the message he bears. The psalms and prayers, on the contrary, remain anonymous: they are made to become the very words of all who repeat them. How can deliberately impersonal texts fashioned for all be considered God's Word?

. . . Is It God Who Speaks?

For want of something better, we could settle for a more or

less satisfactory but still probable explanation: the chants and prayers in Scripture were handed down precisely because of their inner afflatus. Israel detected in them recognizable though often muted tones—faint but authentic echoes of the prophets. And, unquestionably, there is more than just a vague family likeness between the prophetic books and the psalms: there is the presence of a characteristic and immediately identifiable faith. It is the same God, the same nation and the same experiences. Israel's prayers are certainly, in large measure, the fruit born of the Law and the Prophets. From among various and more or less pure fruits, the conscience and faith of this people were able to recognize those which came from the true stock. Thus were the psalms and the other prayers of the Bible gathered together. They, too, in an indirect but legitimate sense, deserve to be called God's Word, for they would not have been born without it.

To be sure, there is some truth in the historical process just described; the genuinely Israelitic features of this or that composition may very probably be what was seen as meriting it a place in Israel's collection of prayers. Still, beyond such likely but unprovable hypotheses, we must lay a more solid foundation—one which we can glimpse better from an episode etched with extraordinary sharpness: Peter's profession of faith at Caesarea.

Peter's Profession of Faith at Caesarea

The Double Question

Matthew's gospel recounts the profession of faith at Caesarea with exceptional amplitude. To Peter's declaration, "You are the Christ, the Son of the living God," corresponds Jesus' symmetrical declaration, "You are Peter and on this rock I will build my Church" (Mt. 16:16–18). The two other synoptics do not follow this arrangement, which is perhaps artificial—a word that does not mean "fictitious." But they begin the same way, with a double question put by Jesus: "Who do people say I am? . . . And you, who do you say I am?" (Mk. 8:27–29). A double question because, as Jesus knows, there are two answers: "Some say [you are] John the Baptist, some Elijah, and others Jeremiah or one of the prophets" (Mt. 16:14). For "the people," Jesus is an enigma—someone with extranatural prestige, like the dead who return to earth or phenomena which transcend imagination. For the disciples, He is at one and the same time greater and more natural: "You are the Christ." This, the simplest reply, the one in Mark 8:29, is no doubt the most literally faithful to the original. Now, right off, it goes infinitely far. Instead of the dazzled stupefaction of outsiders, it substitutes the clear gaze of faith.

You Are the Christ

Before this man and in this situation, to reply "You are the Christ" is, as a matter of fact, to say exactly who He is. Christ is the Messiah of Israel. True, this title is inadequate to define Jesus totally; it can even be equivocal if given only by men, since it may merely signify that they have finally found the face they were dreaming of, the person they were desperately hoping for. For that reason, Jesus is in no hurry to capitalize on it and proves so reticent when they want to bestow it on Him. Yet He cannot refuse it; in fact, He will solemnly claim it before Caiaphas and the Sanhedrin (Mt. 26:63–68) and die for having persisted in doing so. That is because being the Messiah, in the sense in which Jesus Himself understands it, means being the perfect gift of God to His people, the completed expression of His promises, the plenitude of Israelitic personhood—not as Israel conceives and imagines it, but as God wills and produces it. That Messiah—the Messiah of God, as Luke specifies (Lk. 9:20)—is truly the object of faith; He demands of us the very adherence we owe to God, the same total and sovereign fidelity. And it is precisely this fidelity which Jesus recognizes in Peter the moment he says, "You are the Christ."

Situating the Question

As the circumstances surrounding this reply are most significant, the gospels underline both place and time.

The place is Caesarea Philippi, a town outside Jewish territory, and Jesus is there because He has left His own country. He is living in discreet isolation, away from people, since His mission does not extend to the pagans (Mt. 15:24); and if He heals the daughter of the Canaanite woman, that is because He cannot ignore a faith so like Abraham's (Mt. 15:28; cf. 8:11). From this isolation we see how He is keeping His distance from the crowds.

The time is after the miracle of the loaves, which, in all four gospels, marks the moment of the great misunderstanding. A large number of people had come to Jesus with enthusiasm and, thinking they had seen the kingdom of God come that very evening, concluded that they must make Jesus the Messiah (Jn. 6:15). But, brutally frustrating their hopes, He had bidden His disciples (who, no doubt, were quite ready to lead the demonstration) get into their boat, while He dispersed the crowd and retired into solitude and prayer (Mk. 6:45–46). The episode at Caesarea reflects this situation: the crowds vanished, disappointed; the disciples remained, also disappointed, no doubt, but overcoming their feelings.

A Right Answer

Jesus' double question is aimed at both these groups—the throngs on the lookout for prodigies, and the small nucleus of souls closer to Him. The latter give Him the answer He is awaiting: "You are the Christ." For this answer is right, and Jesus can accept it. From the moment it is stripped of illusory dreams, of a hankering for wonders; from the moment it comes into being after trial and crisis, in the naked encounter between a Jesus who is alone and men who have no means at their disposal—then the Messianic ascription is exact and truly says who Jesus is. For Peter and his companions, Jesus as He is at this hour—with all His inner strength and His power over men and things, as well as His visible weaknesses, His deliberate and disconcerting helplessness—is indeed the Messiah of Israel, the promised One whom God is giving His people. And Peter, at the same time as he proclaims this in words, attests to it by his actions, by the fidelity which, through luminous moments and dark hours, has led him, as he followed his Master, to this strange occurrence: the Messiah of Israel recognized by twelve men no one would recognize, in the absence of any public and all publicity, just outside Jewish territory. Enough to ruin the whole enterprise from the start—unless it be the fitting way for faith to acknowledge the form and style of Israel's God.

A Faith-filled Answer

Peter's reply is an act of faith: faith which rests upon Jesus Himself—not His deeds or His mission, but His very person. By a process which is still largely subconscious though already clearly delineated, this amounts to putting Jesus in the place which belongs to God. Never did the prophets ask anyone to believe in them, but always in the divine message they bore. And now Jesus, without explicitly inviting faith or even mentioning it, causes His disciples to make a decisive act of faith, and causes it to be faith in Him.

This act is simultaneously a word and a gesture—a gesture of adherence and a word of proclamation. Both come from a man: from Peter, a Galilean fisherman, standing in the midst of men who identify with his words and actions. These are the fruit of a human experience whose development and stages they could describe; they express a reality which has meaning for the disciples and their acquaintances, the people of that country and that time; they can be repeated, explained and translated; they are the words of men, the words of a religion lived by a nation. What we have here is the experience of a man—not a singular individual lost in his originality, but a man who speaks in the name of his comrades and for the purpose of communicating his experience to others. It is a personal word, found by a man at a precise moment in his life, in order to voice his own experience and distinguish it from many others. It is a spontaneous word, not repeated or learned from someone else, but sprung from the heart and from life. If there is a word which belongs to Peter and his comrades, it is indeed this one, in which they have wholly and entirely placed themselves and committed their lives.

A God-given Answer

Now, this word, uttered and willed by them, does not come from them. Matthew's text is particularly explicit: "It was not flesh and blood that revealed this to you but my Father in heaven" (Mt. 16:17). This "revelation" certainly does not mean a more or less extraordinary phenomenon, voices or visions: Peter would have noticed such things by himself, without any nudging from Jesus. On the contrary, it took place in Peter without his being aware, and Jesus had to make him notice it.

The Work of the Father

What did this revelation by the Father consist in? To a large extent, that is obviously God's secret, one which Jesus knows but does not choose to explain. A constant trait of Jesus is that, while going about His business among men, He remains ever attentive to what His Father is doing in them. John's gospel forcefully underlines that attention: "All that the Father gives me will come to me" (Jn. 6:37); "A child of God listens to the words of God; if you refuse to listen, it is because you are not God's children" (8:47). Sometimes even, at the thought of this mystery which thrills Him, Jesus cannot conceal His amazement and breaks into thanksgiving: "I bless you, Father, Lord of heaven and of earth, for hiding these things from the learned and the clever and revealing them to mere children" (Mt. 11:25). At the profoundest center of the human heart—at the point where God meets His creature, where the Father once again finds His lost children and submerges them in His joy—Jesus is there, present and acting with Him.

Jesus at the Start and at the Conclusion

He is there to tell Peter what God was doing in him; He is there because He Himself brought Peter around to this gesture. Peter's faith is the work of the Father—and of Jesus as well. It is Jesus who called Simon away from his boat and led him through an astounding succession of luminous paths, fearsome horizons and marches in the night. Now it is Jesus who, by asking him this question at this time and in this way, enables him to put that experience together and express it in a decisive act of faith. Lastly, it is Jesus who accredits Peter's reply by confirming the truth of it. Peter was swept along by the impetus and assurance of his fidelity; he felt confident of what he was affirming, but his affirmation becomes a certainty only when Jesus accepts it and recognizes its rightness. Here again, the most explicit of the three synoptics is Matthew: "Simon, son of Jonah, you are a happy man" (Mt. 16:17). But Jesus' strict orders not to tell anyone about Him (Mk. 8:30) are another way of saying that the Twelve have attained to a capital truth and must enfold it in silence, lest it be misinterpreted and misused.

God's Word in Peter

Thus, at one and the same time, Peter's statement comes from him, from Jesus and from the Father. One would think the Holy Spirit is absent, and in fact He is not mentioned—which may be a sign of authenticity. Normally, in the gospels, the Spirit is shown as acting in men only after Jesus' death and resurrection. As long as Christ is present among His own, the action of the Spirit passes through Christ's words and deeds and is indistinguishable from them. The Spirit will be manifestly present only after Jesus' ascension into heaven. Yet the Spirit is at Caesarea as fully as the Father and the Son. The Father gives light, initiates and directs this entire operation; He does so by the visible body of His Son, by the presence and action of Jesus living among men; He does so by the Spirit, who opens Peter's heart to Jesus' invitations and empowers him to formulate the reply Jesus was awaiting—that word of faith.

Peter's Word, God's Word

Given by the Father, elicited by Jesus and born of the Spirit, Peter's word is therefore, because of its origin, God's Word. It is God's Word because of its content, too, because of what it says. When Peter replies, "You are the Christ," he is saying something he has not learned, something he knows without having been told. Jesus certainly did not tell him. It is an essential fact in the gospels—including John's, where Jesus talks about Himself so abundantly—that He is never the first to say who He is. He always waits for others to say it. When this word spills forth from devils, from such as cannot believe, He silences it. When it springs from faith, He accepts it—often with many reservations. And even when solemnly adjured before the Sanhedrin to declare who He is, when there can be no more ambiguity as to the meaning of His titles, Jesus waits and does not take them upon Himself until Caiaphas has given them to Him.

The ultimate reason for His seemingly strange behavior is that this is the only way to reveal truly who He is. Like a professor at his lectern, Jesus could have explained who He was in clear, unequivocal terms. Surely, He was capable of it, and we always tend to think He should have done so, just as we tend to interpret the gospels as if He actually had. But the gospels resist our maneuvers: Jesus gave no lessons and devised no formulas or precise definitions to be parroted at the drop of a hat. As a result, He left faith open to endless discussions and exposed the Church to every heresy. But He established that Church on the only foundation which can hold solid: His own word and her faith. In order to say who He is, Jesus cannot enter into a discourse, however rigorous and objective; for He would thereby be setting His disciples on the path of discourse-and-explanation and reducing Himself to the level of mere nature's products, beings which can be described and defined.

The Word of Faith

Though Jesus does not say who He is immediately but starts by having others say it, He is not using a pedagogical trick designed to stimulate the imagination; instead, He is causing His identity to be proclaimed under the only conditions possible: those of faith—or of faith refused. When He has Peter respond, "You are the Christ," He does not make him find the most complete definition right away but, still, makes him tell exactly who He is. This first declaration does not say it all, and Peter himself cannot yet know how far-reaching is the bond which unites Jesus with His Father and which only His death and resurrection will be able to reveal. But already that bond is inferred and, because of it, Peter can place in the Messiah whom he acknowledges the faith which until then he reserved for God alone. There, to be quite accurate, lies the discovery which constitutes Christianity and distinguishes it from Judaism. Both worship the same God with the same faith, but Peter's faith now finds in God a new mystery, an unsuspected face, a living love, a communion unheard-of and offered to all. In no way could he have learned this by himself, even if he had drawn on all the riches of Israel's faith. He needed to have before him the person of Jesus, who is the living expression of God; he needed within him the depth and drive of the Spirit, who makes man speak to God.

Before the Son and in the Spirit, therefore, Peter's affirmation is truly a word from God. Nevertheless, it comes from Peter, not only because it passes through his intellect and his language and his lips, but because it expresses what is innermost in this man, the mainspring of his life, the direction he has stamped on his journey and his deeds. "You are the

Christ." With these words, Peter discloses the meaning of his life and commits himself wholly and entirely. But these words in which he reveals himself are also wholly and entirely God's word.

Prayer in the Bible: God's Word

Basing ourselves on the central example afforded us in the dialogue at Caesarea, we are now better prepared to understand how the prayers contained in the Bible can really be words from God. Insofar as these prayers are actually responses elicited by questions from God and formulated by men moved by His Spirit, they deserve Christ's approbation: "It was not flesh and blood that revealed this to you but my Father in heaven." Still, such a generalization, if legitimate, poses a delicate problem. What right have we to restrict this privilege to Biblical prayers? How dare we maintain that God has never interrogated anyone but Israelites, or that they alone could answer Him? As a case in point, did Jesus not recognize in the pagan centurion's reply the very faith He expected from the children of Abraham? We might as well say, then, that God speaks in everyone who prays to Him—which is doubtlessly the truth. But what becomes of the Bible then? What should we do with the Book of Psalms but add it to the treasury of human religions?

Until we take up the problem of Biblical religion as a whole in a subsequent chapter, let us here limit ourselves strictly to the domain of the Jewish and Christian Scriptures. Within this domain, clearly, prayer always appears as a reply to an earlier utterance by God. The Israelites' prayer presupposes their election, their deliverance from Egypt, the covenant, the Law given on Sinai. Whether it be thanksgiving or supplication, a triumphal hymn or the confession of sins, it always calls upon the God who has manifested Himself to His people, the God of Abraham and Isaac and Jacob, the God of Moses and the prophets. Even when a prayer assumes the form of a desperate "Why?" (cf. Ps. 22:1), even when Job summons his Creator to answer him and take his side, this audacity and despair cannot spring from anything but faith, drawing their violence and their urgency from the divine face which they once knew and now can neither forget nor blot out. If Job talks to God in such tones, it is because he has learned from God Himself to speak before Him and make himself heard, and God cannot fail to recognize the language He Himself has taught His servants.

Covenantal Prayer

A striking sign of this correspondence between God's word formulated by His interpreters and the word expressed in Israel's prayer, is the very frequent parallelism between covenantal structures and prayer structures. To tell the truth, this parallelism can be explained quite naturally, for covenantal structure necessarily implies an answer from the people accepting the terms laid down by God (Jos. 24:16-24; Ex. 19:8; 24:3). But in more than one passage we can see the parallelism in detail. For example, the promise held out by Nathan and developed along the lines and ideas of the covenant (2 Sam. 7:8-16) is symmetrically matched by David's prayer: "You have done this and this and this. . . . You have constituted your people Israel to be your own people for ever; and you, Yahweh, have become their God. Now, Lord Yahweh, always keep the promise you have made your servant and his House, and do as you have said" (cf. 2 Sam. 7:18-29).

The Circuit of the Word

Even when prayers are not a direct response to the divine word in the covenant, they are still modeled on a response to that covenant. This is the regular pattern for the great prayers in the Bible: Solomon's prayer after the consecration of the Temple (1 Kg. 8:14-53), the mighty prayer at the feast of Tabernacles upon the return from exile (Neh. 9:5-37), the symmetrical prayers of Tobit and Sarah (Tob. 3:2-6, 11-15) and of Tobias and Raguel (Tob. 8:5–7, 15–17), Judith's prayer (Jud. 9:2–14), and Jonathan's (2 Macc. 1:24–29). The great confessions of sin are also structured on this same plan (Ezra 9:6–15; Is. 63:7 to 64:11; Dan. 3:26–45; Bar. 1:15 to 3:8). Each prayer begins by recalling and celebrating the deeds of God and, at the same time, avowing the misfortunes and sins of man. In other words, it begins by listening while God tells His people about their history and their real situation as recounted and interpreted in the Law and the Prophets. Then, in the name of the promises recorded in Scripture, it appeals to God's fidelity. Thus, from beginning to end, Biblical prayer is both the echo of God's Word received by Israel, and the response elicited in man by faith in that Word. This combination of word and response is as ancient as the tradition of Israel. It rests upon the certitude that, "as the rain and the snow come down from the heavens and do not return without watering the earth, making it yield in giving growth . . . , so the word that goes from my mouth does not return to me empty, without carrying out my will and succeeding in what it was sent to do" (Is. 55:10–11). This circuit of God's Word is the whole Bible, it is Peter's profession of faith at Caesarea, it is the entire Church. And, first of all, it is Jesus Christ.

5
Jesus Christ, The Word of God

Jesus is the Word of God; Jesus is God made Word for us. This is a fundamental affirmation of the Christian faith. It could be conclusive proof of that faith's disastrous imprisonment in a religion of book and letter. Instead, it spells decisive liberation: if Jesus Christ is the Word of God, if this Word is a living being, it can never be reduced to mere words, enclosed within formulas, made matter for recitation and repetition. By the same token, it can never be forced into arbitrary frames and prefabricated interpretations. Jesus Christ, Word of God, means liberation from all the barriers erected by language; and He also signifies pure obedience to God, communication—direct and without interpreters—between the children and their Father.

The Word Made Flesh

Jesus was not called "the Word of God" immediately. While living among His disciples, He Himself had never said, "I am the Word of God." And when, after the resurrection, they began to proclaim faith in Jesus and receive believers into their community, they did not at first propose "the Gospel of Jesus, Word of God," but "the Good News of Jesus, Servant of God, the Christ and Messiah sent by God, the Son of God given to the world." The writings which call Jesus the Word of God are posterior to the first years of Christianity and are the work of "theologians," the authors of the letter to the Hebrews or of the gospel and first letter of John. As theologians, these authors seek to understand the faith they profess and to make it understandable to others. In saying that Jesus is the Word of God, they are setting forth an argument and inventing a way of speaking, not for the pleasure of inventing or reasoning, but for the purpose of saying something capitally important about Jesus which no other title could express the same way.

From "Son" to "Word"

When we call Jesus the Servant, the Messiah or the Son of God, we are speaking the truth, but we are not saying everything. We affirm that God and His Servant, His Christ, His Son, are two different persons united by a close and indissoluble bond but necessarily placed opposite each other—the Servant before His Lord, the Christ in the hands of the One who sends Him, the Son come from the Father. Jesus is all that, and His every reaction proves He is constantly attentive to His Father, riveted on His face, drawing from His love.

But there is more between Jesus and His Father than this gaze and this exchange; there is a communion and a meeting which is more than a meeting and more than a union: a oneness. "The Father and I are one" (Jn. 10:30). Not the oneness which can be achieved by dint of love and attention, but oneness from the start, oneness at the origin, indissoluble and indestructible oneness, the blessed impossibility of being elsewhere than in the bosom of the Father: "I tell you most solemnly, the Son can do nothing by himself; he can do only what he sees the Father doing" (Jn. 5:19).

In order to express this unique quality, this privilege peculiar to the Son among all sons—being both the Son opposite His Father, in the fullness of His initiative, and the Son immersed in the fullness of the Father, not separated from Him but, rather, living and breathing in Him—the Christian faith has called Jesus the Father's Word, the Word of God. The Son is Someone other than the Father, but the Word is alive only on the lips of the One uttering it and cannot be detached from Him. If the Son is also the Word, there is a twofold reason: He is Himself opposite His Father, and He is Himself only by never detaching Himself from the Father who speaks.

God Speaks Through the Prophets and in His Son

The letter to the Hebrews helps us understand the road followed by Christian thinkers. Though it does not explicitly call Jesus the Word of God, it does so equivalently: "At various times in the past and in various different ways, God spoke to our ancestors through the prophets; but in our own time, the last days, he has spoken to us through his Son" (Heb. 1:1–2).

The Prophets and Jesus

Nothing could be more natural than to place Jesus in the wake of the prophets. When people address Him, they call Him Rabbi, a title meaning Master or Teacher and commonly used at the time to designate specialists in religious questions. Yet they know full well Jesus is not a rabbi. Rabbis are teachers who have studied under other teachers and are capable of mining treasures from the doctrine of their predecessors. Jesus has no teacher; He repeats after no one. If people do not call Him Prophet, it is because that title is not given by men and does not belong to the vocabulary of human relationships. But, as a matter of fact, by His habit of appealing solely to God's authority, by His freedom of behavior, His singular destiny and His constant referring to His mission, Jesus links Himself to the prophets. And, indeed, at the beginning it is as a prophet that He is received or fought.

Now, what defines a prophet is that he speaks. His very

actions and life-style are always signs intended to reinforce his message. And that message, that word, is not his own. Whether he welcomes it wholeheartedly like Isaiah or resists it desperately like Jeremiah, a prophet always recognizes God's Word because it comes to him from Another. He has no choice but to surrender to it entirely, placing all his intelligence and human assets at its service and drawing upon all the resources of his own speaking ability, though the whole force of the word he utters resides in the fact that it comes, not from him, but from God.

The Message of Jesus, Word of God

Jesus is like that—and yet entirely different. He, too, speaks of God as of Another, and of His message as coming from Another. But one gets the distinct impression that He feels the need of stressing that Other, of having another face appear and another voice resound—the reason being that His own voice is already so clear and His tone so categorical that He commands full attention even without a reference. The prophets do not have to tell us they are speaking in the name of Another, for, however surprising at first, it is instantly obvious. But Jesus' "*I say this to you:* . . ." echoes no one: it springs directly from the speaker; and, to all who truly listen, it offers the Lord's personal guarantee and the immediate experience of Him.

The extraordinary thing about Jesus is that, at one and the same time and in one and the same act, He is wholly and entirely Himself and wholly and entirely the pure and perfect expression of God. He is more spontaneous than anyone else on earth, freer in all His actions, more capable of shaping His own life and leading men down unexpected paths. He does not even need to shield Himself from influences or pressures, since everything He does springs from Him and His inmost heart. But, at the very source of His spontaneity and unalterable freedom, there is the living presence of the Father, together with awestruck joy and grateful pride. That is what St. John means when, at the end of his Prologue, he writes: "No one has ever seen God;

it is the only Son, who is nearest to the Father's heart, who has made him known" (Jn. 1:18). In order to show this perfect and living dependence, this impossibility of being elsewhere than in the Father and of doing something other than His will; in order to show, furthermore, that this immediate meeting is directed toward us, that it is a call and a promise addressed to man, the evangelist adopts the term *Word of God* to designate Jesus. And, in order to show that this Word is indeed Jesus Himself in the fullness of His personality, he makes this name a proper and personal name: the Word.

The Word: a Living Being

Asserting that Christ is the Word of God means unveiling a divine dimension in Jesus. But, at the same time, it means radically transforming the old Biblical images of the Word. The Scriptures open with this statement: "God said" (Gen. 1:3). Abraham, Moses, the prophets, the psalmists and all the great Biblical characters lived in the certitude of having been contacted by a God who spoke to them, had something to tell them and awaited their reply. This certitude was far more than a personal conviction, far more than an experience made precious by being out of the ordinary. Quite the contrary: they recognized one another in a common experience and understood that it was not the mere repetition of an identical phenomenon, but that between all their experiences there was a link, a continuity, a unified forward movement. God's word was not an isolated venture without follow-through; it was a history willed fully, directed firmly and destined for an unimaginable but certain future—the history of a nation, of its birth, its successes and misfortunes, the history of a God consociating with that nation, of His exigencies, His disappointments and promises.

From History to Writing

Because this history had a meaning, because it determined the future and destiny of the generations yet to come, it had to be transmitted and preserved. For that, it had to be engraved in people's memory, so that it might be retold, recounted and sung. In short, there had to be writing and books. Accordingly, God's word, gathered up by faith, became the written word and was read over and over, learned and repeated. This development was imperative and, without it, Israel could not have held on to its faith. But unless the word is constantly received and experienced with faith, it becomes just another text, a pretext for interpretations and commentaries. The Bible becomes a book; and the book, a collection of sayings and quotations for the use of scholars and clergy. The text becomes untouchable and yet susceptible of being cleverly manipulated to justify any and all views.

The Living Scripture in Jesus

But if the Word of God is primarily Jesus Christ, there occurs between the Book and the Person a coincidence which effectuates both the resurrection of the Book and the incarnation of the Person. Everything God produced in the genesis of the universe and the history of Israel, everything He asked of His servants, everything He promised to those with faith—all this leads to Jesus and becomes in Him a living and personal reality. He is the Law and the Prophets: the Law embraced in its totality, understood down to the last iota; the Prophets listened to with an utterly simple heart, followed unto the ultimate fulfillment. But, from that time onward, the Law is no longer the law of Moses, the code of a people separated from others and from mankind: it is the pure will of God, the charter He gives mankind. The prophets are no longer only the heroes of Israel, witnesses to a tradition and a glorious past: they resurrect in their heir, they find the perfection of their message and the plenitude of their vocation in the life and teaching of Jesus. By Himself alone, He is all the prophets, just as He accomplishes the whole Law—not by abolishing them, making their life futile and their message outdated; but, on the contrary, by demonstrating the coherence of all these diverse vocations, the unity of so many pronouncements which seemed to clash together, and the luminous necessity of these opposing messages and torn lives.

The Free Word

The Word, a Person

In becoming a Person, the Word of God acquires both the intangible rigor and the freedom of personal beings. A person is what he is, not as raw material to be manipulated and exploited for profit, but as a living personality, an inaccessible and inviolate mystery. The newborn child, though still completely ductile and susceptible to all kinds of impressions, is already himself and projects the imperious figure of a human person to those who watch him grow. Whether christened Jeanne or Joseph, Paul or Therese, it is the child who gives those names (chosen by someone else) their individual and incommunicable character.

Thus, in becoming Jesus, the Word of God loses none of its authority and gains the distinctness of a perfectly delineated face, of an inimitable voice. Before this unique face and voice, all commentaries and all attempts at adaptation and interpretation betray their falsity. It is impossible to make Jesus say other than He chose to say, impossible to make Him be other than who He is. Not that He is incapable of changing His mind or reconsidering a decision—for He is totally adaptable to circumstances—but He is, at each instant, totally Himself and totally the truth of things and of God.

No Writings from Jesus

Still, because it is identical with the living Jesus, the Word of God in Him is living and free. For Him, Scripture is never a text He latches on to, a document whose every comma must be revered; for Him, even His most personal statements—those which bear His imprint most clearly—are never intangible words. Pilate in his arrogance can uphold the immutable value of the inscription he has had nailed to the cross of Christ: "What I have written, I have written" (Jn. 19:22). Jesus, however, writes nothing, as if to keep all His words and deeds from ever being detached from His person and becoming a sacred missive.

His decision not to write certainly does not come from the fear of being betrayed and misunderstood, nor is it a precaution taken to ensure the possibility of change in the future. Every time Jesus speaks, He commits Himself totally and addresses all generations to come: "Heaven and earth will pass away, but my words will not pass away" (Mk. 13:31). But through all those various words, the one Word must always ring out; and it continues to be the Word only by remaining alive, inseparable from Him who utters it. Because He is the Word of God—of the living God—Jesus cannot become a text.

Word and Text

Yet there must be a text, lest the Word be lost, dying with those who have heard it. It must be transmitted from generation to generation till the end of the world. Hence, it must be written down and given its definitive form. Out of this necessity were born the gospels—the transcription of the words and deeds of Jesus, the Word of God.

In a sense, and more truly than all the other writings in the Bible and the New Testament, the gospels are therefore the Word of God. Still, they are only a secondary and apparently inferior form of that Word, for what seems a conclusive and incontrovertible reason: namely, that the gospels do not contain the words and sayings uttered by Jesus. However shocking this fact may be, we must measure its full import: the words Jesus Himself used have not been preserved for us.

Where Are Jesus' Words?

Jesus spoke Aramaic and talked to people whose mother tongue was Aramaic, a Semitic language related to Hebrew as Italian is to French. And the gospels are written in Greek. The distance between Greek and Aramaic is great, approximately as great as between French and Arabic—which means that no Greek translation may claim to reproduce the original language of Jesus and His first disciples exactly. There is a possibility that Jesus and some of His companions may have known Greek, which was widely spoken in Palestine at that time. But the style of the gospels and of Jesus' utterances proves that He expressed Himself, not in Greek, but in Aramaic, which was the usual language of His country then. There is a possibility, too, that the statements and accounts in the gospels circulated in written Aramaic versions before being translated into Greek. In fact, a tradition not to be ignored, though it must be considerably modified, holds that Matthew's gospel was first composed in Aramaic. Be that as it may, when we assign to Aramaic sources the key role in the formation of the gospels, we always come up against a notable fact: none of these sources has survived, and the text of the gospels—the sacred book of Christians—is a translation. We barely have a few of the Aramaic words Jesus used. Of these, the most precious and the only one whose loss would have been irreparable is *Abba*, the word (equivalent to our "Dad") which He instinctively chose when speaking to His Father. Quite likely, He Himself had, as a little child, invented this language to voice His spontaneous experience of God.

The almost total disappearance of the words Jesus used is obviously no accident. It forms part of the Jesus event just as fully as the date of His birth or His training for manhood at Nazareth. In one sense, it is even far more important. Had Jesus grown up in some other Galilean village but Nazareth, He would have become rather much the same man He did. But the fact that the gospels and the New Testament were written in Greek is uniquely and crucially significant.

A Necessary Gap

In a certain way, this creates a historical gap, an unbridgeable chasm between Jesus and us. To rediscover His sayings in their literalness, we Christians—even those of Jewish descent, those closest to Him by reason of blood and culture—must proceed indirectly, making detours through the scientific realm of history and languages. Far from being fruitless, our detours may yield us much precious information about Jesus. But they cannot substitute for faith properly so called, which receives Jesus' teaching, not directly in the original, but as His early followers received it.

Though this gap seems an obstacle, it is really an essential safeguard. Thanks to it, the gospels give us the Word of God in its living reality. If they were the immediate transcript of Jesus' words as He spoke them in His language, then the text itself would enjoy priority and He would simply be the author of it. Then, too, the Aramaic text would be the authentic word, and the translations would necessarily be but deficient approximations. That would automatically create two categories of Christians, one of which, by birth or education, would have direct access to and instinctive comprehension of this prototext and inevitably impose its own interpretation on everyone else. The Word of God would thus be reserved to a privileged few.

A Salutary Safeguard

Instead, since the gospels in their original form are already translations, they can always be translated into other languages without these other languages being considered inferior. This is precisely where the work of translators and exegetes becomes so meaningful in the service of the Christian people. For science and comparative linguistics can go beyond the Greek translations and establish texts which are closer to the original, thus facilitating other translations truly capable of rivaling the Greek. Although the Greek remains the sacred text, the original and the norm for all translations, it is itself only a particular form and privileged expression of the Word of God. And even the Aramaic text—if ever it comes to light again—would still not be the Word of God, but only one expression of it.

The Word and Words

Jesus alone is the total and perfect Word of God. And because Jesus is a man, none of His sayings suffices to express Him entirely. Each of them states God's truth exactly, with the authority and unerringness of divine vision. But each is born of a specific situation and designed to answer a specific question. Consequently, we should not be surprised that even the gospels contain statements which are difficult to reconcile—as, for example, "Do you suppose that I am here to bring peace on earth?" (Lk. 12:51) and "Peace I bequeath to you, my own peace I give you" (Jn. 14:27). In order to understand them, we must put them back in their context. Above all, we should never detach them from the personality of Jesus and the totality of His life.

Jesus Christ is the unique and perfect Word. But even the Word cannot yield itself up entirely in one word, in one sentence or, for that matter, in a series of discourses. Jesus needs His whole existence, needs His life and His death to say everything He came to tell us. That is why the profoundest fidelity to the Gospel, the closest listening to the Word of God in Scripture is never just literal repetition. Faith heeds the Gospel to the letter, careful not to distort or sugarcoat its message. But it does not make the letter an idol, an untouchable object. The only untouchable, absolutely sacred being is the person of Jesus Christ. Listening to the four gospels and knowing the evangelical dicta inside out is insufficient and delusive unless we keep our eyes riveted on the living person, unless we contemplate the Lord directly. The singular value of the gospels and the proof of their authenticity lies in this: that they always forbid us to separate the words spoken from Him who speaks them, the words from the Word.

6
The Word and Scripture

"We believe that the Bible is the Word of God." This proposition is basic to the Christian faith. But it can also be an ambiguous maxim, where all the words are falsified and lose their meaning. Such ambiguity, one must admit, is not so very rare; and those who want to be most scrupulously faithful to the Scriptures run perhaps the greatest risk of falling into it.

The Ambiguity of Literalism

Ambiguity is always spawned by literalism, by the illusion which mistakes literal reading for spiritual understanding, the text for the Word. The Word of God had to be gleaned and fixed in writing, for this Word—pronounced and received at a given moment in history, at a particular point in the development of mankind—was addressed to all peoples and constituted a cardinal event for the entire human race. Hence, it had to enter into human systems of communication and transmission; it had to become Scripture. Even so, it must always remain the Word spoken and heard, a dialogue between living persons. Short of that, it becomes a mere collection of memories handed down to uncomprehending heirs. The tribe of critics tear it to shreds so as to remake it to their liking, while the bulk of the faithful stand guard around it like a treasure in a museum.

Literalism and critical arbitrariness, it must be added, can coexist. In the same church one may hear the same voice quote a sentence from Scripture as if it had been uttered by God Himself, and then refer patronizingly to essential Biblical pronouncements on the mortal danger to which sin exposes us or on the reality of the risen Jesus. In order to take Scripture seriously without turning it into an untouchable relic, we have to understand how the Word of God becomes Scripture and how, in Scripture, believers receive the Word.

The Word and Scripture

"When he had finished speaking with Moses on the mountain of Sinai, he gave him the two tablets of the Testimony, tablets of stone inscribed by the finger of God" (Ex. 31:18). According to this undoubtedly ancient tradition, the decalogue, the heart of Israel's Law, was engraved on two stone tablets by God Himself. A later account has Moses writing down the words of the decalogue for the people: "Moses went and told the people all the commands of Yahweh and all the ordinances. In answer, all the people said with one voice, 'We will observe all the commands that Yahweh has decreed.' Moses put all the commands of Yahweh into writing" (Ex. 24:3-4). Later still, the prophet Isaiah is given a message to transmit, which closes with a precise piece of information: "I bind up this testimony, I seal this revelation, in the heart of my disciples" (Is. 8:16). A century after that, God says to Jeremiah, "Take a scroll and write on it all the words I have spoken to you about Jerusalem and Judah and all the nations, from the day I first spoke to you, in the time of Josiah, until today. Perhaps when the House of Judah hears of all the evil I have in mind for them, each man will turn from his evil way, and then I can forgive their misdeeds and their sin" (Jer. 36:2-3). Almost at the end of the Jewish Scriptures, the

Book of Ecclesiasticus concludes with a sentence we would nowadays use as an introduction: "Instruction in wisdom and knowledge has been committed to writing in this book by Jesus son of Sira, Eleazar, of Jerusalem, who has rained down wisdom from his heart" (Sir. 50:27). At first glance, the evolution seems clear: God writes, Moses transcribes, Isaiah seals a message, Jeremiah gathers up years of preaching, and Ben Sira shares the fruit of his reflections. With time and the advent of the critical spirit, what was once attributed directly to God became a manifestly human achievement, resulting from the work of man.

It would be naïve, however, to let ourselves be taken in by this simplistic scenario. For there was an evolution in the opposite direction, too: over the centuries, writings which bore no sign of coming from God or of having been composed at His bidding and under His influence—such as Ecclesiastes or the Song of Songs—acquired the status of sacred books and were ranked with the more ancient works, like the Law, where God speaks in person.

The Law

Actually, without denying this visible evolution and these changes in language, we must, above all, understand the variations which occur when God is made to speak. They obey a profound and solid logic. In matters of the Law, God speaks directly to the whole of Israel and to each Israelite. This is so evident to the hearer that there is no need to add, as the prophets will later, "Thus says Yahweh." And when God wants to tell about Himself, He always does so in the first person and without quoting: "I am Yahweh your God . . ." (Ex. 20:2; Lev. 18:2, etc.). That is because there exists a strict coincidence between God and the authority Israel obeys. What gives the Law its sacred weight, what renders it indisputable and makes every transgression a sin in the proper sense of the word—an offense against God—is the fact that, in the Law, God expresses His will categorically. As a result, obedience to the Law derives from the personal relationship between man and God and pertains to the realm of dialogue properly so called. To obey is to say "Yes," to disobey is to say "No"; in either case, there is a response to an order, to Someone who speaks.

The Prophets

If, on the contrary, the prophets have to keep repeating "Thus says Yahweh," that is because their message does not of itself command attention with the same authority as God. It bears the personal seal of each prophet, it addresses itself to a situation which is always different and singular, it is leveled at such and such a person or category of persons, it has meaning today and will lose it tomorrow. God does not speak there as in the Law. And if the prophets, to justify their interventions, must so frequently recall their vocation and the instant when God seized them, it is precisely because their own words take up such a large part of their message that we may ask whether they leave room for God to speak. For us today, the incomparable value of the prophets lies in meeting men who live out their individual destiny and stamp their efforts with their own personality. All of them, however, in their several ways, reiterate that, if they are sent to speak and must pour all their human resources and inmost self into their message, they are there only on orders from God and can say only what He commands them to say. They are not the Word but servants of the Word and, in their own way, speak what the Word tells them.

The Sages

Still more astounding is the case of the writings grouped under the general title of "wisdom books." Here, the speaker—who is manifestly not God—most often goes unnamed. The brand of wisdom best represented is the anonymous wisdom in Proverbs, the immemorial wisdom of the nations. It derives its savor and value from the fact that it gives intensely vigorous and striking expression to truths which are rooted in common experience and immediately win everyone's assent. The "authors" of this literature accurately describe themselves as compilers dedicated to collecting the most complete and meaningful examples of it. Even Qoheleth, whose voice is the most personal of all and who feels compelled to raise it in protest against certain untenable views, writes under the name of Solomon. In so doing, he is neither using a transparent pseudonym nor attempting to lead the reader astray, but simply following the convention of a well-defined literary genre in which the author has no personal merit unless he succeeds in reflecting a universal experience.

How can we maintain that this essentially anonymous voice is God's and that these experiences, which possess worth only because everyone has undergone them, are communications from on high? Must we resort to slogans like *Vox populi, vox Dei*? That would be tantamount to saying that God does not speak but that, in order to hear Him, we must listen to men—the very opposite of what the Biblical and Christian tradition holds: namely, that the wisdom writings, just like the Law and the Prophets, are directives from God.

Wisdom Personified

To extricate ourselves from this impasse, we need only look more closely at how the wisdom writings are organized, and we shall see that all or almost all of them—the major ones, at any rate—suddenly bring forward a majestic and mysterious figure, Wisdom speaking in person. In Chapter 28 of Job, its presence and action are both the world's inaccessible secret and a mystery which God reveals to those who fear Him. In Proverbs 8 and Ecclesiasticus 24, Wisdom itself lifts up its voice and begins to speak. But its voice sounds exactly like God's and its teaching enjoys the sovereign authority of Him who gave the Law. There is no doubt that this entire tradition—while never mistaking Wisdom for God, since it is created—hears God speaking personally through the voice of Wisdom.

The Articulation of These Literary Genres

How explain this new, paradoxical fact? The only answer is quite clear and far-reaching.

Through the Law (and what is both ethnically singular about it and profoundly human, as in the decalogue), Israel receives God's Word in its most immediate form: a destiny which is special to this nation but which, far from being fated, is rather a permanent call to be answered each day. That is where God, down the ages, unceasingly speaks to His people and makes them exist as a community of faith.

In the Prophets, it is the same God who speaks, using their experience to give His face, His heart and, therefore, His message a new and unforgettable urgency. Yet, their most beautiful exhortations would be but incoherent cries unless they took up their places at either side of the Law to uphold it and probe its full meaning. Because they are at the service of God's Word, they enable Him, in the Law, to speak to His people ever more forcefully and specifically.

Wisdom, lastly, shows where the Law is to be applied—over an area as vast as mankind. Without its sapiential books, Israel would be a nation cut off from the rest of humanity, isolated and incapable of sharing its experience; with them, the Law is lived by authentic people, people with a culture of their own, who know what life is and can communicate their knowledge to others in the language of the day. Conversely, these wisdom writings allow the world to understand Israel, to get its bearings from Israel's unique experience, and to realize that it is itself being called.

Thus we see that, although He speaks in such different ways, the speaker is always God. On one condition, however: that the Law, the Prophets and Wisdom never be separated. When isolated from the Law, the Prophets may be outstanding witnesses to God, but they cannot help us understand what He expects or how we should reply. When isolated from the Law and the Prophets, Wisdom may be a precious testimony to an ambitious and lucid attempt at understanding man and the universe in relation to God, but, of itself, it is no longer God's

Word. His Word makes itself heard in many ways; still, it is unique and is really understood only if heard as a unique call.

Inspired Writings

Revelation and Inspiration

Perhaps these reflections will shed light on a few notions as essential as they are easy to misinterpret. First of all, on inspiration with regard to Scripture. It is a truth of faith and a basic tenet of Christian consciousness that the Scriptures are inspired by the Holy Spirit of God. Furthermore, the Church in our day has solemnly defined that this inspiration extends to the Scriptures in their totality and in their every detail. Wishing to exclude from His divine action such passages as might seem shocking or provably false would be illusory.

So stated, this truth often sounds absurd and indefensible. That is because the word *inspiration* can be ambiguous. We generally take it to mean a form of poetic or artistic inspiration, in which a creator feels that the work he is producing is given to him as if it came from elsewhere. And indeed, if the Bible, a work composed by men, is at the same time the Word of God, it, too, has literally to come from elsewhere. But there is no reason why God, that Other who lives elsewhere, must use what we normally call inspiration when He would speak to men. A poet like the author of Job or a prophet like Isaiah certainly experienced some degree of inspiration in our sense of the word; but if they are inspired by the Spirit, it is on another score and in other modes, which pertain to faith. Scriptural inspiration is that action of God's which causes a chronicler to do his job as chronicler, moves a poet to write poems and impels a prophet to carry out his prophetic mission, in such a way that these various authors taken together—though some may clash and some may not always see the big picture—mark out the road God has taken to speak to His people and elicit a response from them. Necessarily global, the Spirit's inspiration empowers every Biblical author (whether known or forever anonymous) to compose, each in his own capacity, the literary corpus called "the Bible," the literature and culture of Israel. That same corpus gave birth to Jesus Christ and those who understood Him and announced His coming. Since the whole of Israel's experience contributed to forming the humanity of Christ, everything in the Bible is necessary—as were the thirty years at Nazareth, where, through contact with people, He learned about human life, found out what it meant to be a Galilean and acquired the local accent. There is a parallel between Scriptural inspiration and the incarnation. The same Holy Spirit who shaped Christ's body and humanity with the cooperation of the Virgin Mary, her body and her heart, used the sacred writings of Israel to shape Christ's religious vision, His way of looking at things and events, of speaking to God and men.

Hearing God Speak in Scripture

If God speaks on every page of Scripture but in such a different vein, we must, in order to understand Him, be sensitive to the particular tone of each passage, open to the manifold calls of the Spirit, and free in our attitude toward the "letter" of the text. For the temptation to idolize the "letter" is always present—for some, because they invariably think of authority as rule-making and look upon books as manuals to be memorized or formularies to be repeated; for others, because they are always ready to read their own views into a text and then impose them on everyone else; and for others still, because they are animated by the spirit, not of faithful attachment, but of contestation, almost refusing to accept the text as it stands. But this refusal is yet another form of slavery, an interpretation which never manages to welcome the Holy Spirit.

Hearing God speak in Scripture is both a human operation, involving intelligence and attention, and a spiritual one, involving adhesion to God. The intellect has its role to play, since the Scriptures are productions of man, of a language and a culture. To know what a particular author or book was trying to say, we have to know how people wrote and spoke at that time. But there is still greater need of recapturing the faith of the author and his public, of listening to him in the secrecy of our room, since God is the one who is speaking and awaiting a personal reply. In addition, we must hear Him in the midst of His people, in His Church, for the Bible is, first of all, God's word addressed to His people.

Your Word, O Lord, Is Truth

The truth of Scripture is one of the most burning, most painful issues of the current crisis in the Church. For a long time, the presence in the Bible of statements which are manifestly false by the usual criteria was a scandal to be kept hushed; gradually, it became a glaring fact which simply had to be admitted; and, today, it is common knowledge for a great number of Christians. At what a price, though! That discovery has proved to be an inexhaustible source of distrust toward authority—an attitude which terrifies some and fascinates others. When the most sacred thing in the world, God's Word, is shown to be riddled with fallacies, whom can one trust?

This turmoil simply results from a series of misunderstandings. For the most critical minds today, if illuminated by faith, God's Word in Scripture remains unshakeable Truth. But, to understand it, we must loyally welcome the purifications imposed on us by criticism and faith. The truth of the Scriptures in their diversity passes through the truth of the different kinds of language they contain. The truth of Scripture in its totality consists in the oneness of the spiritual experience which constitutes it and which is the genesis of Christ among mankind, the genesis of belief in Christ by His people and by the Church.

Truth from Different Areas

"The genesis of Jesus Christ"—such are the opening words of Matthew's gospel: its title, we might say. This genesis pre-ents what is primarily a genealogical list of Christ's "ancestors," but the list also summarizes the whole of Israel's Scriptures in a few lines. Now, these Scriptures are the history of Israel and its origins as lovingly recalled through the centuries. What produced Christ was a long chain of events lived by a people and still living in their memory, an ethic and a law, a culture and a life-style, a varied, contrastive and sometimes contradictory experience of life and the world. The Scriptures would be false if they reflected but one model, if they offered but one point of view. Their truth results from giving each of these diversified expressions its rightful place and creating a coherent whole.

The Truth of Faith

This coherence comes from within; this unity comes from the Spirit. The profound truth of Scripture is essential Truth, which is the person of Jesus Christ, Son of God. Even in the gospels, there are diverse kinds of exactitude. Infancy narratives, accounts of the Passion and testimonies about apparitions of the risen Lord obey quite different rules. We cannot discover the truth by lopping off the variety of these styles and reducing them to a uniform skeleton. Quite the opposite: we must maximize the characteristics proper to each style—the density of the infancy narratives, the linear severity of the Passion chronicles, the simplicity of the apparition stories—so that, from these various angles, we may bring into focus the authentic features of Jesus Christ, the concrete reality of the Christian experience. We come to the truth of Scripture, the authenticity of Jesus' face and the purity and integrity of Christian belief, not by eliminating difficult texts and awkward facts, but by achieving a synthesis which is careful to let nothing be lost.

7
The Word of God and the Church

For many people, for many Christians, there is an enormous distance—unbridgeable, perhaps—between the Church and the Word of God. The Word of God is a call, an invitation to reciprocity and communication; the Church is a system, an institution which commands attention, an authority not to be gainsaid. The Word of God is a gentle voice, on the borderline of silence; the Church (whether through the mouth of those who govern her or through the din raised by all who feel called to speak) is a discordant tumult, a jumble of languages that cannot come to terms, of voices trying to drown each other out. How, amid this deafening roar, can anyone detect the "still, small voice," the whispered words God enables us to hear only in deepest tranquility?

Yet, the Church was born of God's Word, born to reply to it, to transmit it and make it heard in our hearts. Between the Church and the Word, there is no opposition but, on the contrary, a profound kinship, an immediate and primordial juncture. To separate them is to drain the Church of her lifeblood and rob God's Word of all real efficacy.

The Church Hears the Word

Proof that God spoke to Abraham is the fact that, having heard that voice, Abraham set out, built his life on God's command and gave birth to an undeniable reality: the children of Israel, the nation of believers. Proof that God spoke in Jesus Christ is the fact that Christ called certain men to gather around Him and follow in His footsteps; and that these disciples—after their Master's death and disappearance, and despite their limitations and their inadequacies—founded, within the Jewish world, a community of believers capable of facing death, surmounting persecutions and maintaining its originality down through the ages, and of doing so in response to His initial bidding: "I have chosen you . . . Go . . ."

In the Man Jesus Christ

In these signs, there is far more than a divine force able to overcome obstacles; there is the meeting of a call from God and adhesion by man. Now, we have here a definition of the Church. First and foremost, the Church is this decisive event: namely, that the Word of God in its pure and perfect form, in its matchless originality and plenitude—the person of Jesus of Nazareth—has been received and recognized for what it truly is: the only Son of God made man. Not only decisive, this event is unique and unprecedented as well. For, at some point or other in their life, countless people grow conscious of a message from God, of a call and the response they must make; but they do not constitute the Church, since each call remains personal and particular. Very often, however, such calls extend beyond the individual, since no one can exist apart from his human milieu; but even when God, while speaking to one man, reaches a multitude—as in the typal case of Abraham, with whom a whole nation identifies for generation upon generation—there is still no question of the Church, since, for all these people, God's Word continues to be the one addressed to their father and remains inseparable from him. The Church comes into being when God's Word exists corporeally in the man Jesus Christ.

The Church, Created to Recognize Jesus Christ

Some people, heirs of Abraham by blood and faith, have been capable of this decisive leap: recognizing the presence of God in the man with whom they had lived, whose human origins they knew, whose conduct had so often jarred and disappointed them, and whose future (even after His resurrection) eluded all their expectations and dreams. They recognized in Jesus the perfect expression and the authentic face of the ineffable God. Without these men and without this faith, Jesus would have been just another man of God in this world—the greatest, perhaps—but His true identity would have remained unknown, God's Word would have found no echo, and the incarnation would have served no purpose. These men and this faith are the Church. It is not the Church which discovered Jesus Christ and penetrated His secret. It is the Father who revealed to Peter the truth about His Son (Mt. 16:17), and no one comes to Jesus unless the Father draws him (Jn. 6:44). But, in the same act in which He sent His Son, God was also creating the Church, since He was giving Jesus the hearts which would recognize Him through faith.

The Bride and the Voice of the Bridegroom

The secret which constitutes the Church is to know Jesus Christ, to receive in Him the love and the gift of the Father. This secret is nuptial, making of the Church the Bride and Body of Christ. It reaches fulfillment in the Word she receives and the faith she extends. If God gives His Word in Jesus Christ, there has to be someone to receive it, and so He creates the Church. Here, everything takes place beyond images, beyond dreams and feelings. At the heart of reality, at the center of the world, there is Christ, the Word of the Father, and, next to Him, the Church His Bride.

"The bride is only for the bridegroom" (Jn. 3:29). What makes bridegroom and bride is the fact that they draw together in mutual knowledge, at a secret depth safe from alien eyes. The closest friends remain apart, and the truest are filled with joy at this mystery which, though accomplished outside their ken, nevertheless crowns their fellowship. So it is with John the Baptist when Jesus begins to reveal His power over hearts. But those who have known Jesus and answered His call cannot forget this experience: "Lord, to whom shall we go?" (Jn. 6:68). Once we have given Jesus our faith—"We believe; we know" (6:69)—we can only betray Him or remain with Him; there is no possible place we can go without Him.

The Church Where We Hear the Word

The Church is the Bride, and yet she is not a real person. She is a reality of the personal order, since Christ loves her and speaks to her, and since she hears and answers Him. Still, she is not a person; she has no real existence independently of her members. How, then, can we say she hears the Word of God? How call her a bride except through poetic or lyrical imagery? And how claim that she can demand faith?

In truth, if we try to give the Church a personal face according to our own models, we end up in all sorts of impasses. The most common and most natural, from the moment we portray her as a person who speaks and makes decisions, is simply to identify her with those within her who speak out and make the decisions—that is, essentially, with the priests and the hierarchy. But this singularly narrow perspective does not explain the reality.

The reality is that the Church is the place where we hear the Word of God in the form it has assumed in order to embrace all mankind: the person of Jesus Christ. Believing in Jesus is the act of individuals, not of a Church which would exist above them; but this act is possible only in the Church and through the faith common to her members.

Beyond Individual Experience

The reason is this: if Jesus Christ is the Word of God addressed to mankind, we cannot receive that Word and believe in it through an experience which remains singular. If Jesus were just a message sent to me personally, I would merely have to assimilate this experience and establish between us a relationship known to God alone. In a burst of generosity, I might even tell others about it; but it would remain my personal experience, as Islam is the experience of Mohammed and Buddhism of Buddha. But when Jesus comes, He presents Himself as heir to the tradition and hope of Israel. That tradition and hope had universal import: Israel was the nation apart, but it had been chosen so that its victory might also save humanity and restore the whole of creation. To receive the revelation of God in Jesus is to believe that He brings the crucial event in the history of the world. No individual experience can elicit this faith.

The Church, the Proper Reply to the Word

That is why Peter, when declaring at Caesarea that Jesus is the Christ, or when announcing in Jerusalem that the risen Jesus is the Messiah of Israel and the Savior of the world, always speaks in the plural, in the name of a community. This plural includes his immediate companions, the circle of the Twelve, first of all; but they themselves do not claim to be voicing only their personal experience. To proclaim that Jesus is the Messiah is automatically to summon the entire Messianic people, convoking them so they may hail their King. To say that this Messiah is the Son of God is to make a statement which has no meaning unless it is true for everyone, for all who profess to adore the true God. However small at birth, in numbers and importance—twelve ordinary men, provincials without education or prestige—the Church, from her first words, speaks as heritrix of Israel and its faith and welcomes God's supreme gift to the world. Outside this faith common to the people of God, outside this universal perspective, it is impossible to recognize who Jesus is or really understand His being and His mission. Outside the Church, there is no faith in Jesus Christ, no proper reply to the Word of God.

The Word Received in the Church

There is a difference between receiving the Word *in* the Church and receiving it *from* the Church. If the Word is the Son of God, God alone can give it. The Church is the place where this Word is recognized, where it takes on its meaning, and no one can work out his own interpretation by himself. Just as we must use words in the same sense as everyone else when expressing ourselves verbally, and just as violence inflicted upon language succeeds only if the public understands and countenances it, so a believer's experience of Jesus Christ finds meaning and expression only in the faith community which is the Church.

But the very experience of the Word, the presence of Jesus with His personality, the challenge of the Gospel, the invitation to contemplate and follow Him, all of which is the Word itself at its source, the living person of Jesus—all this comes, not from the Church, but from elsewhere: from God Himself. The Church's role is to point out this Other and this Elsewhere, to attest that she is not the Word but is there to receive and hear it. Everything the Church says, every word she addresses to the world—and her duty is to speak: "We cannot . . . stop proclaiming what we have seen and heard" (Acts 4:20)—all this strikes listeners the more forcefully as they perceive in it the echo of another Word, the need to make it heard, the desire to respond to it.

The Gospels and the Word of God

The Church must speak; but, in speaking, she must see to it that the Word of God, the person of Jesus Christ, comes through with all its power and its unique ring. A difficult task, this—humanly impossible. But the Church has been able to do it, thus proving she was born of God. The first token of her successful response is the gospels.

A Distance . . .

The gospels are not the Word of God in the exclusive and strong sense of the term, since that Word is Jesus Christ, the Word of God made flesh. As we saw in the preceding chapter, they are all translations and present Jesus' words and deeds only indirectly, through the memory and meditation of the first witnesses, through the reflection and elaboration of the authors who composed these four accounts. From one book to the next, there are many differences and, at times, discrepancies which the evangelists make no attempt to conceal. This only points up the role played by individual viewpoints, deliberate purposes, subconscious assumptions—in a word, by the personality and the private world of each writer.

In one sense, all these particularities, all these consecutive processes of meditation, composition and translation establish a veritable distance between Jesus and readers of the gospels. Immediate contact with Jesus was, for those who lived it in faith, something unique and unforgettable. The author of the first letter of Saint John (and undoubtedly of the fourth gospel) cannot erase from his memory "[what] we have heard, and we have seen with our own eyes; [what] we have watched and touched with our hands: the Word, who is life" (1 Jn. 1:1), the Word of God.

. . . Which Is Not an Obstacle

But John does not conclude that this unique gift is forever inaccessible to those who were not there. Quite the contrary, he writes in order to announce "what we have seen and heard . . . so that you too may be in union with us, as we are in union with the Father and with his Son Jesus Christ" (1 Jn. 1:3). The distance is not really an obstacle. Between those who have seen and those who have not there can be a communion so profound that it introduces us all into the communion between the Father and the Son, God and His Word. This communion goes so far that those who have not seen can even surpass those who have: "Happy are those who have not seen and yet believe" (Jn. 20:29).

There is, therefore, for those who have seen and heard the Lord, something to do and say. What has taken place before their eyes should not remain a personal memory to be jealously nurtured. Because it was the Word of God, it must speak to the entire world. And because this Word was silenced with Jesus' death and is nevertheless risen and living, it must be given the means to speak again till the end of time. This speaker has to be man, for it is by becoming man that the Word reaches men, and by living and acting as man that it has yielded itself up to us. As a consequence, we need to go back to Jesus' words and the life He lived. One essential feature of the gospels is that they constantly have Jesus speaking: all those who speak around Him are there to draw Him out and make His words clear.

The Gospel According to John

John's gospel is the best example of the work proper to evangelists: making Jesus speak. This gospel of the Word of God obviously flows from a long process of elaboration and personal meditation which gives the words of the Johannine Jesus a characteristic and inimitable accent almost entirely missing in the synoptics. Whence the rather natural suspicion that these words are but creations of John's. As a matter of fact, many of them probably are, but we have to be sure we understand the nature and meaning of this procedure. It signifies that an evangelist's meditation consists, not in inventing, but in listening. For Jesus continues to speak. But in order to listen to Him speaking thus, one has to have heard Him already. Just as anyone who would serve as a witness to the resurrection has to have been present "the whole time that the Lord Jesus was travelling round with us . . . until the day when he was taken up from us" (Acts 1:21–22); so, too, if an evangelist would continue to hear Him speaking after the resurrection and learn from the Spirit the profound meaning in His words of yesteryear, he has to be borne up by the breath of Pentecost until he rediscovers in the experience lived by the Church the pristine voice and the human face of the Jesus who used to dwell with His disciples.

John's gospel—the "spiritual" gospel—remains a gospel because it never separates the Spirit from the Word and because, in it, the Spirit enables us to hear and understand what the Word used to say. The evangelist of the Spirit is also the evangelist of the Word of God, the evangelist of Jesus. Jesus speaks, and the Spirit comes, not to hush Him, but to help us more fully grasp the significance of His words.

The Synoptic Gospels

What strikes us in John's gospel also appears, less systematically but just as really, in the three others. All four were written to link the action of the glorified Christ with His human experience. All four rest on the conviction that, to receive the Word of the risen Lord, we must hear it as it was once uttered. This work of piecing material so as to insure continuity can be done only in a spirit of constant dependence on Jesus, His words and His deeds. That is why, in a rigorously true sense, the gospels are the Word of the Lord. More exactly still, they contain it and hand it on, not as a shapeless gangue from which we must extract precious stones, but as texts wholly governed by concern to transmit the Word and communicate the experience and faith of the witnesses. The gospels impart the Word of God because they impart the faith of those who first were called and seized by that Word and responded to it. The gospels are the supreme example of what constitutes all the Scriptures: the Word of God expressed in the words of man. In all the other cases, however, the Word of God is not isolable, and man can mix much of his own material into it. The evangelists likewise have put a great deal of themselves in their work, but what they have put in especially is their attention and their faith; and that is why, despite the poverty of their means, they have succeeded in sketching the unique face of Jesus and making the living Word of God into a real, living man.

The Church and the Gospel

The New Testament Is Complete

This faith, this attention, this encounter with the living Word is the Church—the Church living in the heart of men, making four evangelists out of them and bringing them to compose their gospels. The gospels came into existence in the Church; that is a historical fact and also, more profoundly, a certitude of faith. They are one of the purest expressions of the Church at her birth: discovering the person of Jesus, gleaning His message, living by His death and His Spirit.

The Church went through this experience once and was born of it. She cannot repeat it: once the witnesses have died, no one can write a new gospel. Nor can anyone even relive Paul's situation or Peter's or that of the New Testament authors—the very men entrusted with establishing and spotlighting the fundamental bonds between Christ and His Church. With the generation of the apostles, the Word of God found full expression: the New Testament is complete.

The Word of God and the Word of the Church

God cannot speak without eliciting a reply: "Yes, as the rain and the snow come down from the heavens and do not return without watering the earth, making it yield and give growth . . . so the word that goes from my mouth does not return to me empty, without carrying out my will and succeeding in what it was sent to do" (Is. 55:10–11). God's will must be done not merely in external events but in the human heart as well. When the Word came into the world, it evoked faith from Peter and the Twelve and caused the Church to be born.

The apostles' response, the first response of the Church—the one through which she came into being by discovering who she was—is again the Word of God; and this for two reasons: first, because this Word is born (so to speak) of the tête-à-tête between Jesus and His disciples; and, second, because the presence of Jesus, of His concrete personality, of a face which cannot be disfigured and a voice which cannot be imitated guarantees the rightness and truth of their response. The New Testament period, when witnesses can still immediately perceive the relation between the pre-Calvary Jesus and the risen Jesus, between Jesus living among His own and Jesus reigning as Lord of the Church—that privileged period is the day of the Word.

God Continues to Speak

That period comes to an end when the generation of witnesses, the apostolic generation, dies out. But God does not, for all that, cease to speak. Although He has sent us His Son, although He has communicated His Word to us, we should not conclude that He has nothing left to say and can only repeat Himself, referring us to what He has already said once and for all. If, on the contrary, He has granted us His Word, He wants to assure us that He will never stop speaking to us, for His Word is living and goes on living eternally. But everything He says to men, to those who have received the Gospel proclamation, He says so that they may rediscover it in the total truth of His Word, in the person of Jesus Christ.

Thus, the Church is the community of those who, gathered together by the Gospel and the name of Jesus in the power of the Spirit, live this earthly life in the Gospel and the Spirit. The Church is of today; today she receives the Spirit, who makes all things new; she receives Him from the Father through the Son, who delivered Himself up to death in order to give Him to her. What the Spirit tells her today is always a call toward the future, a new discovery. At the same time, it is always something known, something she has heard before, something she keeps hearing in the Gospel, something in which she rediscovers the voice and accents of her Lord. And what she hears today, she must tell and announce. That is why she speaks.

The Church's message is one, yet multiple: there is the dogmatic message of the bishops, who speak in virtue of their office and authority; there is the prophetic message of the martyrs and saints, who bear witness to the Gospel; there is the daily message of those anonymous Christians who, from generation to generation, transmit the faith they have received; there is the message of faith rising from Christians gathered in prayer; there is the message of charity and hope from those who toil, looking after the poor and the despondent. However different, all these messages blend into one, for there is but one Spirit. However human, they spring from the Spirit and the Gospel. They are not the Word of God—that unique Word—but they all echo it and render testimony to it. The Church has to speak, has to teach, act, pray and give thanks. If she grew silent, it would be that she no longer heard the Word in her heart. But she must also know when to keep still and invite us to silence, so that we may perceive the voice which is softer than any words—that mysterious voice: the Word of God.

8
The Word and the Sacrament of Reconciliation

Since the Word of God is primarily the Father's Eternal Son made flesh and blood for us, made words and deeds, made a human existence in our midst and a life laid down and raised up again, it is inevitable that this Word cannot communicate itself entirely through words, however precise they may be. A word given is true only if kept.

When the Son—God's Word given and kept—appears on earth, He brings to it both the Father's words and deeds. The Gospel announces an event: the kingdom which is coming. The Beatitudes announce a gift: the joy Jesus brings to those who have nothing. This joy and this kingdom cannot be just words; they have to be realities given and lived.

The Initial Gift: Forgiveness

As soon as Jesus starts proclaiming the Gospel, the first gift He brings is forgiveness. That is His specific mission; and, after

John the Baptist's arrest by Herod, it impels Him to leave the Jordan and baptism by water and go into Galilee to announce the Good News (Mk. 1:14; Jn. 3:22–24; 4:1–3).

This glorious news is that God forgives. In the past, the prophets had often preached forgiveness; and, though sent to denounce Israel's sins and warn of consequent destruction, they never totally lost sight of God's pledge: "I will betroth you to myself with faithfulness, and you will come to know Yahweh" (Hos. 2:22); "Though your sins are like scarlet, they shall be as white as snow" (Is. 1:18); "They will all know me, the least no less than the greatest . . . since I will forgive their iniquity and never call their sin to mind" (Jer. 31:34); "I shall cleanse you of all your defilement and all your idols" (Ezek. 36:25). When rousing his followers to conversion, John the Baptist remembered all that; and, when baptizing them, he declared that the promised hour was near and, indeed, about to ring. But he could go no further: he was but a voice and a promise.

From John the Baptist to Jesus: from Promise to Forgiveness

Jesus likewise speaks, proclaiming the Gospel throughout Galilee. But He gives what He promises: He brings God's forgiveness. That is why He has come—to call sinners and afford them pardon. He proves it by His miracles, which show that God has empowered Him to forgive (Mk. 2:1–12); He proves it by His demeanor, His habit of welcoming sinners, especially those whom society ostracizes—the publicans and the prostitutes (Mt. 21:31); He proves it by the miraculous purity which transforms the hearts that draw near to Him (Lk. 7:36–50; 19:1–10; 23:39–43).

This way of acting not only astounds but scandalizes His fellow Jews, who cry, "He is blaspheming. Who can forgive sins but God?" (Mk. 2:7). Jesus does not contest what is for Him, too, a fundamental truth. He comes purposely to show that, with Him, it is God's forgiveness which is being offered to sinners, and that the gesture of the Son of Man on earth is the gesture of God in heaven (Mk. 2:10).

Your Sins Are Forgiven

There is something perhaps even more unmistakable than all these signs which are so expressive of forgiveness; I mean the very words Jesus uses when granting it to someone: "Your sins are forgiven you" (Lk. 5:20–23; 7:48). This is a personal statement, addressed personally to a definite person, in a concrete situation. It refers to sins which have really been committed and which will remain a secret between God, Jesus and the forgiven sinner, although the formula is uttered in public and everyone within earshot knows this is a case of a real sinner and a real absolution.

The formula may vary: "I do not condemn you" (Jn. 8:11); "This man, too, is a son of Abraham" (Lk. 19:9); "Indeed, I promise you, today you will be with me in paradise" (Lk. 23:43). Whatever the wording, the facts and their purport remain the same: a truly guilty man or woman, placed beyond the pale of society because of transgressions, is publicly forgiven by Jesus and presented as an example to all—like saying, "See what God's forgiveness and the action of the Son of Man can produce."

Christ, Sacrament of the Kingdom of God

Here, the Word produces its full effect. Here, the Gospel is no longer just a promise, but an event: communication with God is restored, salvation has come, love has borne its fruit. The notorious town prostitute and Zacchaeus the tax collector, the woman caught in adultery and the crucified thief have all been purified and made into new creatures, and the kingdom of God is now present in the world.

These men and women are still but signs, scattered faces in the crowd. They impress those they meet but do not necessarily convince them. They themselves, moreover, though conscious of the transformation in their life, have not yet gone below the surface of the forgiveness they have received or of the love which inhabits them. In many respects, the pardon Jesus bestows exhibits the properties of the sacrament, of an action of

God's in a still opaque world where His presence remains unseen. That action is real, the transformation undeniable and visible in its effects. It is produced by a word which possesses the efficacy of the creative act and therefore carries the power of God. It unfolds in the midst of the world, before the eyes of men, of those who are ready to believe, those who take scandal, and those who do not know what to think. Sacrament, public gesture, bringer of a spiritual happening, sign expressed and explained by a word . . . By taking flesh in our humanity, the Word of God becomes the primordial Sacrament: the incarnate Word gives rise to the event known as "the kingdom."

From Christ-as-Sacrament to the Sacraments of Christ

The Sacraments, Gestures of Jesus Christ

Jesus' action does not cease with His death. On the contrary, now that He is no longer limited by the barriers of the mortal body, His action henceforth extends to all creatures, and His resurrected body becomes His Church. Though present throughout the universe by the power of the Spirit, this action finds within the Church the place where it is proclaimed and signified, the place of the Word and the sacraments. In the Church, Jesus continues, through the transmission of the Scriptures, to announce the Gospel and the kingdom of God. In the Church, He continues, through the sacraments, to bring us the Father's gift—the Holy Spirit. And in the Church, we discover what we receive from God and learn how to respond to Him.

Since the Church's sacraments draw their meaning and reality solely from being the action of Christ, and since they are nevertheless gestures executed by men, these gestures must enunciate two facts: that it is the Lord who acts, and that man can act only in His name. The sacraments always comprise a word; and it is both the Word of the Lord, the efficacious Word of the Gospel and the kingdom, and the word of the Church, the word of the minister who acts in the name of the One who sends him.

And I Absolve You . . .
in the Name of the Father and of the Son and of the Holy Spirit

The sacrament which most clearly shows the link and the distance between the Word of Christ and the word of His minister is the sacrament of forgiveness. God alone can forgive; and Jesus, when forgiving sinners, did not take God's place. The formula He used—"Your sins are forgiven you"—signified with utter clarity that the unexpressed subject of the action was God Himself. In Jewish apocalypses, the impersonal passive was frequently employed to designate God without pronouncing His name. This device is one of the characteristics of Jesus' style; thus, "Happy those who mourn: they shall be comforted" (Mt. 5:5) really means "God will comfort them." When He told the harlot or the paralytic, "Your sins are forgiven you," Jesus, speaking as man but also as witness to the secrets of God, was revealing to men that the Father was in the process of granting His forgiveness. Confessors may recite the formula of absolution, but they are not Christ, for they possess neither the lucid spiritual gaze which He trained on the depths of man's heart nor the immediate access to God which made His words the very Word of God. They can speak only as men, trying to judge a situation and understand someone else's conscience. Yet, in the name of the Lord who sends them, they can repeat the divine word of forgiveness to those who seek them out.

The Sacrament, a Word Received

Like Jesus' words in the gospels, the word of forgiveness in the sacrament is usually personal and actual. It drops from heaven at this present moment, on a conscience fully aware of having done evil. Everyone needs to hear that "his sins" are forgiven him. Of course, he cannot separate this forgiveness from the one which has come to enfold "all our sins," and it is also good for him to hear "Your sins are forgiven you" spoken in the second person plural; but both forms are necessary.

The sacrament of reconciliation is nothing other than the evangelical word of forgiveness. It is the only way this word can remain a real word, a personal communication, and not be reduced to a memory of an inner call. For the word in the Scriptures is not only the word which holds true throughout the ages of the eternal God; it is the word which goes on living till the end of the ages of the risen Christ. And because it goes on living, because it is ceaselessly born of the heart of a man resurrected so He may remain a man for God's eternity, this word becomes a sacrament and is spoken to me today through a confessor.

I may, in the Gospel, hear the story of the sinful woman or of the Passion and then apply Jesus' statement to myself: "Your sins are forgiven you." Or I may hear a priest tell me, "I absolve you." These are two different experiences. In both cases, it is the same word, the same forgiveness and the same Gospel. But the Gospel is not only a word which I must make my own through faith; it is a word which I must, with faith, receive from another. God is that Other, the Wholly Other. God, incarnate in Jesus Christ, is the Wholly Other become man in order to speak to me. The sacrament which places me before someone else—before a priest—causes the Word of God to remain that of the Other and my words to remain a response.

9
Where Does God Speak?

Outside Scripture and the Sacraments

God speaks to us in Scripture and in the sacraments, which keep this Word living and present. But must we hold that God does not speak outside the Scriptures? Many people consciously base their life-style on a call they honestly believe to be the voice of God. Must we say they are deluding themselves? Must we adjudge that this call could indeed have meaning for them (since nothing escapes God's watchfulness and governance), but that these individual cases belong to an altogether different order from the official and authorized Word of God?

Must we therefore believe that, apart from privileged groups—that is, Jews and Christians—the vast majority of mankind (whether the countless billions before Abraham or those after him but outside the Judeo-Christian tradition) has not heard and cannot hear God speak to it? Or, since it seems difficult to prevent God from communicating with creatures fashioned in His image precisely so He might speak to them, must we drastically dilute the concept of *word* and strip it of any real relation to the authentic Word of God given in Jesus Christ?

And what must we think, then, of those Christians who claim they find the Word of God in the fabric of their daily life, in the quotidian routine and, more particularly, in exceptional manifestations of courage and generosity? Does not the liberation of a subjugated people literally duplicate the birth of Israel? What of the impulsion which gives rise to movements of resistance and solidarity among the downtrodden masses? Is this not the contemporary form of the Acts of the Apostles? And, surely, the invitations heard by today's Christians as they gather to pray to the Holy Spirit are the very same as were heard in the Christian communities of Caesarea or Antioch.

A God Who Speaks

To shed light on these questions, we should first of all open the gospels and listen to Jesus. Now, from everything He says, it becomes evident that the God of Jesus Christ is a God who speaks and who says far more than we hear in the Scriptures and the gospels.

In the Sermon on the Mount, Jesus says, "When you pray, go to your private room and, when you have shut the door, pray to your Father who is in that secret place" (Mt. 6:6). Obviously, He supposes that God, under these conditions, will speak to the individual in question and that He has something to tell him. And how can we maintain that that man belongs to a particular race, to a definite religion? Jesus certainly did not come to teach that one creed is as good as another. But what He says here, He patently says about each man and for all men. In the very name of the Gospel, it is correct to affirm that God speaks to everyone and awaits a reply from all.

When Jesus marvels at the faith of the centurion who has come begging that his servant might be healed, He finds in this pagan the very faith He is having so much trouble rousing among His own people—the faith of Abraham and Isaac and Jacob (Mt. 8:10–11). In the name of the Gospel itself, therefore, we must infer that God spoke to this pagan as He had once spoken to Abraham, and that the Roman officer obeyed as Abraham had.

When Jesus calls His disciples' attention to a poor widow who has just put her last penny into the alms box (Mk. 12:44), He shows them how God can make Himself heard by the simplehearted.

The entire Gospel reveals to us a God who speaks, a God whose utterance is true because it is not merely a flux of words, and because He is also a God who looks and listens, who calls and waits. In the name of the Gospel, we must conclude that, wherever there are human beings, God is there to make them hear His Word.

Where Is the Privilege?

Where, then, is the privilege enjoyed by the people of God? Where is the unique originality of the Scriptures? The gift reserved for the Church? Why keep our eyes fixed on the generation of the first disciples, so far removed from us? Why worry about preserving texts which have become incomprehensible? If God speaks today, let us strive to hear Him today.

The truth is this: between the Word of God, which took shape in the Scriptures and became the flesh and blood of Jesus Christ, and the word God continually addresses to us throughout our life, there is not only kinship but true identity. What He tells us now in no way differs from what He told the people of Galilee through Jesus. What He tells the Chinese is simply the Gospel of His Son. But He says it to each nation in its own language and culture, to each individual in the realities of his life, to each era in its dramas and dreams. Because God has truly spoken to His people in Jesus Christ, we know He wants to speak to all men.

This does not allow us to affirm categorically that a particular act or event is, as such, the Word of God. The sole Word of God, in the full sense of the expression, is the person of Jesus Christ. All the Scriptures contain and speak this Word, since, between them all, they say who Jesus Christ is. Outside the Scriptures and their expression in the faith and sacraments of the Church, everything we experience at the inmost core of our life is an encounter with the God who speaks to us. Among all these encounters, a great many go unheeded, and a few serve as models. But not one of them is entitled to the status reserved, because of the incarnation of the Word, to the person and expression of Jesus Christ.

Nor can any of them replace Scripture and the Church. But all, if authentic, have an affinity with Jesus Christ and the Gospel. The saints produced by Christianity, those most acutely conscious of not being the Christ (cf. Jn. 1:20) and of not speaking the Word of God, are also the very ones whose kinship with the Gospel is most manifest.

What Criteria?

Outside Christianity, the true God is present and speaking along the well-known roads of the religious world and the unnamed paths traveled by the masses. A Christian, however, should neither believe that "the Christ is there" (Mk. 13:21) and espouse all kinds of pseudo-Messianism nor turn his back on mankind, which God loves in its entirety. The more he listens to God speak to him in the Gospel, the better he can perceive and help others perceive, in other languages and entirely different situations, the same voice of God, the same faith response from man. The Word of God recognized in Jesus Christ is the criterion which should permit all His followers to authenticate the numberless messages God addresses to His children. This authentication is the work of the Spirit. Many wish for objective criteria to assist them in deciding whether a given act or event is or is not a communication from God. The very notion is fraught with danger. Certainly, there are criteria; or, more exactly, there is but one criterion: kinship with Christ, evangelical authenticity. This criterion is objective, as the person of Jesus Christ is objective; but it can be seen only in the light and action of the Holy Spirit. If we are resolved to view a particular decision or initiative or way of acting as the expression of a word from God, we shall succumb to the temptation denounced by St. Paul and substitute our works and our successes for God's work—faith. Rejecting the label "word of God" is the way to let Him speak and dispose ourselves to hear Him.

Appendix
To Get the Most Out of this Book

A. Important Books on the Subject

Pierre Grelot, *The Bible, Word of God: A Theological Introduction to the Study of Scripture*, translated by Peter Nickels (New York: Desclée Company, 1968). The fullest discussion of "the Word of God" and related questions. Solidly grounded on an exceptional knowledge of Scripture as well as clear-sighted fidelity to the Christian tradition, and keenly aware of current problems, the author skillfully uses insights from earlier times to blaze new trails.

Jean Levie, *The Bible: Word of God in Words of Men*, translated by S. H. Treman (New York: P. J. Kenedy, 1961). Like Pierre Grelot, Jean Levie was both an exegete and a theologian. His book, though less complete than Grelot's, is more directly centered on the relation between the Word of God and human speech. The development is both logical and historical. Having himself lived through most of the period from the start of this century and the Modernist crisis down to the convocation of Vatican II, Levie takes up all the pertinent questions as they were successively raised, debated, dodged or solved. The result is a history of both exegesis and Catholic theology on this subject for the first half of the century.

Georges Auzou, *The Word of God, Approaches to the Mystery*

of the Sacred Scriptures, translated by Josefa Thornton (St. Louis: B. Herder Book Co., 1961). Not as didactic as the two preceding, not as weighed down with references and not as rich in precise information, this work is nevertheless both solid and suggestive. Its personal tone and often savory intuitions make it easy and lively reading.

Dom Célestin Charlier, *The Christian Approach to the Bible*, translated by Hubert J. Richards and Brendan Peters (Westminster: The Newman Press, 1965; New York: Paulist Press Deus Books, 1967). In a simple way and without technical apparatus, this book, too, presents basic notions about the Bible together with the questions they raise. Most particularly, it highlights the spiritual riches of the text and the central place Christ holds in understanding Scripture.

Henri de Lubac, *The Sources of Revelation*, translated by Luke O'Neill (New York: Herder & Herder, 1968). On Christ's place at the center of the Bible (our Chapter 5) and on the reading of the Bible in Church (our Chapter 7), this book, in less than 300 pages, gathers up the whole of Christian tradition in language nourished by our whole Christian past and yet immediately accessible today. Especially valuable will be the sections on "the act of Christ" and on "the fact of Christ."

Luis Alonso-Schökel, *The Inspired Word, Scripture in the Light of Language and Literature* (New York: Herder & Herder, 1972). A research tool on the fundamental processes of expression and literary creation. Somewhat more difficult than any of the volumes above because it presupposes rather broad knowledge, it goes to the very bottom of the problems. For those who wish to delve deeply into the subject, this is both an introduction to essential areas and an invitation to further discoveries.

B. Guidelines for Individual or Group Study

1. *For Chapter 1 and the expression "God speaks"*

In the Book of Genesis, find the various formulas which say, in one way or another, that "God speaks." List them homogeneously: "God said . . . ," "Yahweh said . . . ," "The

Word of God was addressed to . . . ," "Yahweh appeared . . . and said . . ."

Instead of asking (which is pointless) whether these formulas denote different experiences among the characters in question, try to define the context and style of the passages where these diverse formulas occur.

See whether each of the lists includes a response from man and what kind of response it is: a sign of obedience, an act of faith, a cultual gesture.

2. For Chapter 2 and the covenant

Compare Gen. 9:8–17 and 17:1–22 with the structures mentioned in this chapter (Ex. 19–24; Deut. 1–27 and Jos. 24). Find the parallels between the composition of the two passages from Genesis; see whether this parallelism is found in the broader structures of Exodus and Deuteronomy.

Compare the sabbath law in Ex. 20:9–11, in Deut. 5:12–15, in Lev. 23:1–3 and in Ex. 31:12–17. Notice the different rationales presented. Ponder why the sabbath is part of the decalogue and why, unlike the other commandments, it needs justification.

From the gospels, jot down Jesus' remarks concerning the sabbath, showing exactly how they reflect the Old Testament and exactly how they transcend it. Do not forget Jn. 5:9–18.

Compare the structure of the covenant in the Old Testament with that of the New. In particular, study Lk. 22:14–30 and Jn. 13:1–35, and try to detect, in both passages, a movement analogous to that of the Sinai covenant: the past, the present and the future, the place of ordinances and their justification.

3. For Chapter 3 and the prophets

As against the experiences of Amos described in this chapter, compare the calling of Isaiah (Is. 6), of Jeremiah (Jer. 1:4–19; 20:7–10) and of Ezekiel (Ezek. 2–3). Observe how God's word, far from being received passively, mobilizes all the personal resources of the prophets.

Study Peter's discourse in Acts 2:14–39. See how Peter echoes Jesus' message announcing the Gospel and how, nonetheless, far from repeating Jesus' phraseology, he creates a new language. This language, too, is the Word of God.

4. For Chapter 4 and the prayers of the Bible

In 2 Sam. 7, notice how David's prayer mirrors Nathan's prophecy, verses 18–29 corresponding to verses 5–17.

See how the major confessions of sins (Neh. 9; Bar. 1:15–3:8; Dan. 3:26–45; 9:7–19) are structured on the three moments of the covenant. To the divine utterance describing what it has done in the past, there corresponds the sinner recalling God's deeds; to statute and ordinance, there corresponds admission of disobedience; to God's promise for the future, there corresponds supplication that He may remember His promise.

Compare the thanksgiving in Ps. 104 and the creation account in Gen. 1. That thanksgiving results from contemplating God's work as produced by His word.

Search the Bible to discover how each petition of the Our Father originated in a statement from God.

5. For Chapter 5 and Jesus Christ, the Word of God

Observe how Jesus adopts the various styles used in the Old Testament to speak in God's name: the language of injunction and commandment (Mt. 5–7; Jn. 13 and 15), the language of wisdom (the Beatitudes, the practical counsels in Mt. 5–7, the parables in Mt. 13), the language of the prophets (the threats in Mt. 23, the warnings in Mk. 13, the promises in Jn. 14–16).

Then observe how Jesus modifies and transforms these modes of expression and how He utilizes what was said before Him, whether in the name of God or on the basis of some human experience.

Note, in particular, how His words of forgiveness (Lk. 5:20–24; 7:47–50; 19:9; 23:34–43) show that He is conscious of voicing God's own word.

6. For Chapter 6 and the written Word

From Ex. 24:4–7; 34:27–28; Deut. 27:3 and Jos. 24, where Moses and Joshua write down the words of the Law, try to determine why they do so.

Why, in Ex. 24:12; 31:18 and 34:1, is it said that God Himself writes His words on tablets? What does this gesture signify?

Ascertain from Is. 8:1–4, 16–20 and 30:8 why Isaiah is ordered to write. Compare Jer. 30:2; 36:1–32; Ez. 4.

Does Jesus write? Why not? Why, on the contrary, does Paul write and attach importance to his letters? Read 1 Thess. 5:27; 2 Thess. 2; 1 Cor. 5:9; 14:37; 2 Cor. 2:13; Gal. 6:11; Col. 4:16.

Read Chapters 3–5 of Vatican II's Dogmatic Constitution on Divine Revelation, *Dei Verbum*, looking up the Biblical references.

7. For Chapter 7 and the relation between the Word of God and the Church

Study Chapter 5 of the Dogmatic Constitution *Dei Verbum* with the help of Henri de Lubac's *The Sources of Revelation*.

On the basis of Peter's and Paul's discourses to the Jews (Acts 2:14–39; 3:13–26; 4:10–12; 5:30–32; 10:36–43; 13:17–41), study how the language of the nascent Church takes shape from rereading Scripture in the light of the Jesus event—that is to say, how the Church discovers her specific message in the Word of God.

8. For Chapter 8 and the discernment of God's Word in events

Here, it is less a matter of study than of practicing such discernment. However, there is benefit to be gained from two sources: from the gospels (especially Jn. 14:25–28; 16:1–33), where we see the perspectives Jesus proposes when promising the Spirit; and from Acts (1:15–26; 2:14–21; 4:23–31; 10:24–33, 44–48; 11:1–18; 15:5–21), where we see how the leaders of the nascent Church discover both the action of the Holy Spirit and the meaning of Scripture.

C. How All This Changes Our Life Today

If God really speaks to us, we must learn to listen to Him.

What does "listening to God speak to us" mean?

First of all, it means a basic attitude of receptivity, of attention—in other words, a constant readiness to set aside our viewpoints, our pet ideas and our personal convictions. Just as we learn to know others only by watching them act, listening to them talk and empathizing with their joys and sufferings, so we hear God speak only when we are willing to forget our own habits.

Listening to God speak does not mean waiting for extraordinary signs, hoping to be brusquely seized by some impulsion or illumined by a sudden revelation. God has endless ways of speaking to the human heart. Most often, He speaks to us through the events in our life, through the people we meet— provided we do not undergo these experiences passively. God speaks to us through our reactions: He gradually shows us in what respect they are limited or inadequate and in what respect they can have positive value. God speaks to us if we are alive; but living is not merely budging and manipulating people and things: it is also keeping still, listening, preparing ourselves.

Listening to God speak means also—and always— listening to Him speak in Scripture, especially in the gospels. And it means perpetually going from the Word offered us in the Bible and Christian tradition to the word received personally in the secret of our heart and the banality of daily life.

The Word of God presented in the Bible comes first— because it is the experience, not of an individual, but of a people forever watched over by God; and because, ultimately, it is the very experience of Jesus Christ, the one He inherited when He became man among the Israelites, the one He lived in the presence of His disciples and thus communicated to His Church.

Today, when all traditions, even the most ancient and solid, are severely shaken and called into question as man inquires into his destiny, his past and his future—today, more than ever, listening to the Word of God becomes a requisite for the Christian life, an indispensable basis for any kind of spiritual life. Not that we want to overlook human events by substituting the Word of God, but that, on the contrary, the Word of God is never more human than in the Bible. Nowhere else is the wealth, the weight and the depth of the human experience so densely concentrated. To deepen our knowledge of the Bible, to let ourselves be taught by the Scriptures, is both to learn the art of listening to God and to discover what man is.

Listening to God speak in the Scriptures means taking Him utterly seriously. If God speaks, it is because He has something to say, and woe to anyone who would disregard His Word! But listening to God attentively implies trying to understand what He wants to tell us through these books written by men. Understanding Scripture is not a matter of memorizing every page of the Bible word for word, but of learning to move with ease through this vast world and explore this garden of wonders. That includes the ability to spot the large trees, the dominant features, as opposed to secondary plantings and common vegetation. For there is no garden without all these things. On the other hand, we must not falsify the proportions.

Hearing God speak in Scripture means taking our own place in the Church. The Scriptures are addressed to the Church first, and it is in listening to God speak to her that she has gathered and consecrated the Scriptures. To hear them within the Church is both to heed a voice which is not ours and comes from elsewhere, and to discover that, by listening with the Church, we train our ear and catch the Word of God more distinctly. The Church does not deliver the secret of the Scriptures to us by dint of explanations and elucidations. She listens and teaches us to hear. She looks and teaches us to see.

Learning to listen to God in Scripture means liberating ourselves from false conflicts, from pseudo fidelity to the letter-as-idol. But it also means tirelessly digging ever deeper, realizing that even our closest attention will never have finished exploring this treasure. Just so, love keeps discovering the features of a face which is always new, always inexhaustible—the face of the Lord Jesus.